Graphic Medieval History

CASTLES

By Gary Jeffrey & Illustrated by Nick Spender

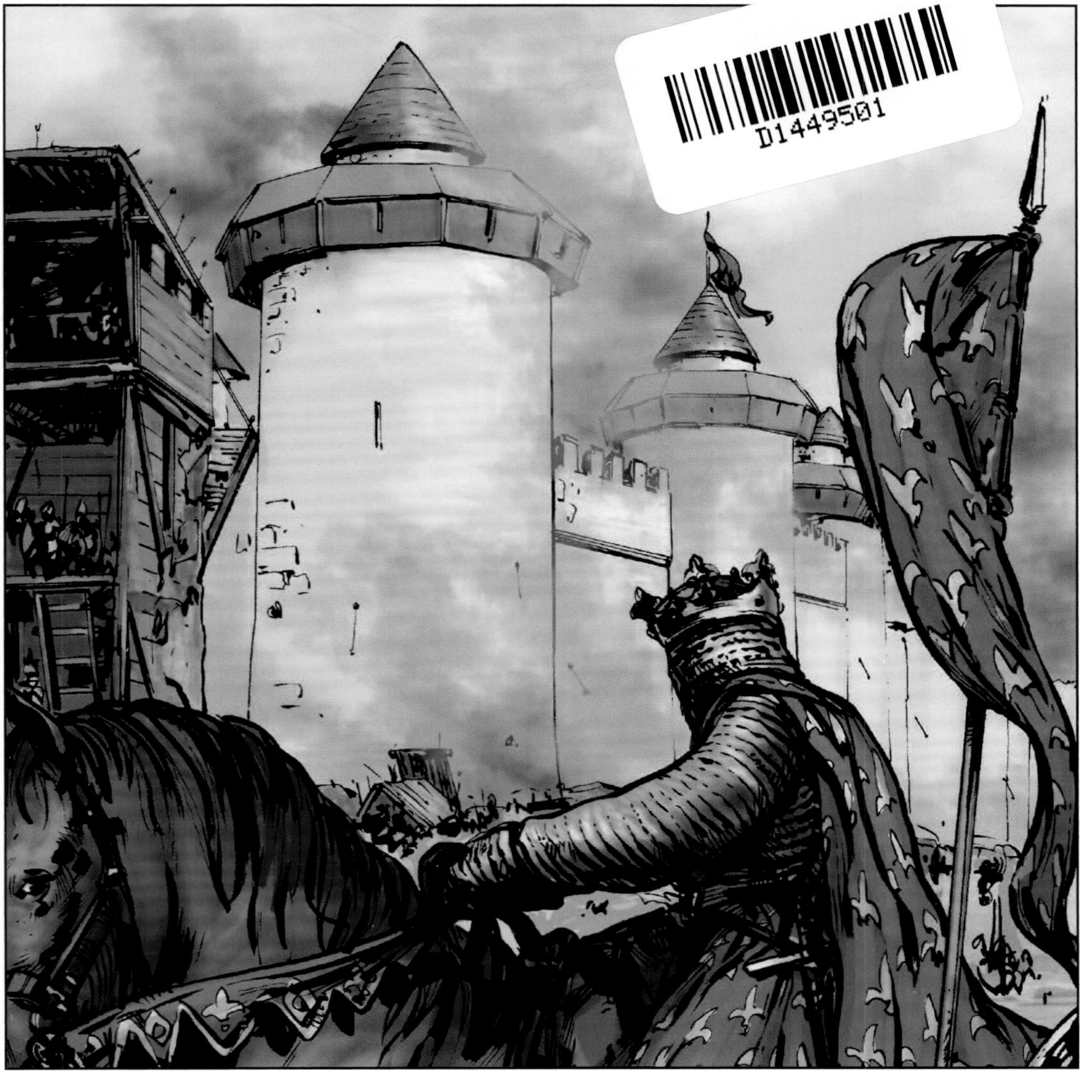

Crabtree Publishing Company
www.crabtreebooks.com

Crabtree Publishing Company
www.crabtreebooks.com
1-800-387-7650

Publishing in Canada
616 Welland Ave.
St. Catharines, ON
L2M 5V6

Published in the United States
PMB 59051, 350 Fifth Ave.
59th Floor,
New York, NY 10118

Published in **2014 by CRABTREE PUBLISHING COMPANY.**

Printed in Canada/032014/MA20140124

Created and produced by:
David West Children's Books

Project development, design, and concept:
David West Children's Books

Author and designer: Gary Jeffrey

Illustrator: Nick Spender

Editor: Kathy Middleton

**Production coordinator and
Prepress technician**:
Ken Wright

Print coordinator:
Margaret Amy Salter

Photo credits:

p5m, David Dixon, p5b, Jonaslange;

p6, ChrisO; p7m, Clem Rutter, p7b,

derek billings; p44m, Humphrey

Bolton; p45t, Jerzy Strzelecki, p45m,

Michael Hanselmann, p45b,

PHGCOM; p46, Tequask; p47,

Antony McCallumi

Library and Archives Canada Cataloguing in Publication

Jeffrey, Gary, author
    Castles / Gary Jeffrey ; illustrator: Nick Spender.

(Graphic medieval history)
Includes index.
Issued in print and electronic formats.
ISBN 978-0-7787-0396-9 (bound).--ISBN 978-0-7787-0402-7
(pbk.).--ISBN 978-1-4271-7508-3 (html).--ISBN 978-1-4271-
7514-4 (pdf)

    1. Château Gaillard (Les Andelys, France)--History--
Juvenile literature. 2. Dover Castle (Dover, England)--History--
Juvenile literature. 3. Conwy Castle (Conwy, Wales)--History--
Juvenile literature. 4. Château Gaillard (Les Andelys, France)--
History--Comic books, strips, etc. 5. Dover Castle (Dover,
England)--History--Comic books, strips, etc. 6. Conwy Castle
(Conwy, Wales)--History--Comic books, strips, etc. 7. Graphic
novels. I. Spender, Nik, illustrator II. Title. III. Series: Jeffrey,
Gary. Graphic medieval history.

UG428.J45 2014   j725'.1809409022   C2014-900355-2
                                         C2014-900356-0

Library of Congress Cataloging-in-Publication Data

Jeffrey, Gary.
  Castles / by Gary Jeffrey ; illustrated by Nick Spender.
    pages cm. -- (Graphic medieval history)
  Includes index.
  ISBN 978-0-7787-0396-9 (reinforced library binding : alkaline
paper) -- ISBN 978-0-7787-0402-7 (paperback : alkaline paper) -
- ISBN 978-1-4271-7508-3 (electronic HTML) -- ISBN 978-1-
4271-7514-4 (electronic PDF)
  1. Castles--Europe--Juvenile literature. 2. Middle Ages--
Juvenile literature. I. Spender, Nik, illustrator. II. Title.

  UG428.J44 2014
  355.4'40940902--dc23

                                      2014002417

Contents

Castle Building

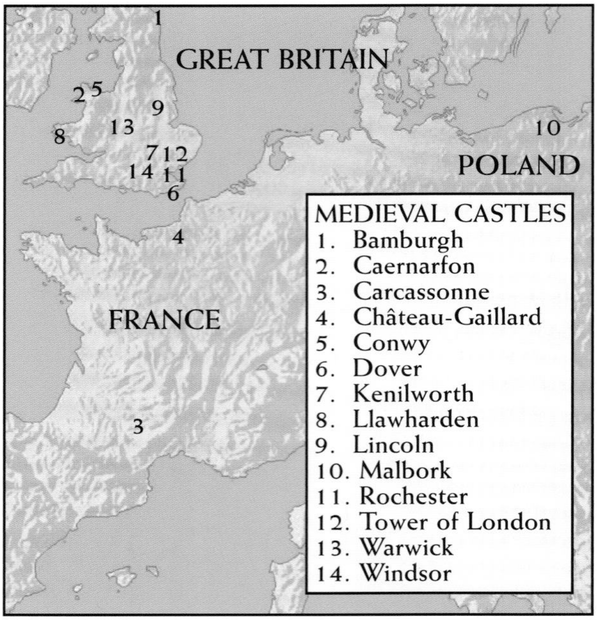
GREAT BRITAIN
POLAND
FRANCE
1
2 5
9
13
8
7 12
14 11
6
4
3
10
MEDIEVAL CASTLES
1. Bamburgh
2. Caernarfon
3. Carcassonne
4. Château-Gaillard
5. Conwy
6. Dover
7. Kenilworth
8. Llawharden
9. Lincoln
10. Malbork
11. Rochester
12. Tower of London
13. Warwick
14. Windsor

Military forts and walled towns had existed since ancient times. In the 9th century, when the vast empire of the Franks split into smaller territories called lordships and principalities, private landowners started building their own castles.

Motte and Bailey

In France during the Middle Ages, early castles had a keep, or tower, built on a raised mound of earth called a motte. The tower acted as a guardhouse or residence for the lord's family. Next to the motte a large, flat yard, or bailey, was built for stables, storerooms, and other buildings. The entire complex was surrounded with a palisade, or a fence of wooden stakes, and a ditch to protect against attack. A small force of permanent soldiers lived there too. However, rot and fire were the main enemies of motte and baileys.

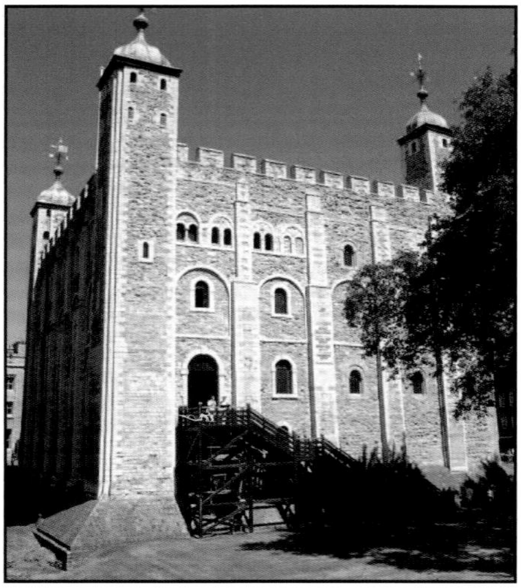

The massive Norman keep at the Tower of London was William the Conqueror's fortress in London.

Castle Keep

William of Normandy conquered England in 1066. The Normans built their castles all over Britain and even rebuilt important wooden ones in stone. The main keep, or donjon, was a fortress. Some had incredibly thick walls. However, most castles back then only needed to be strong enough to hold off an attack until help arrived.

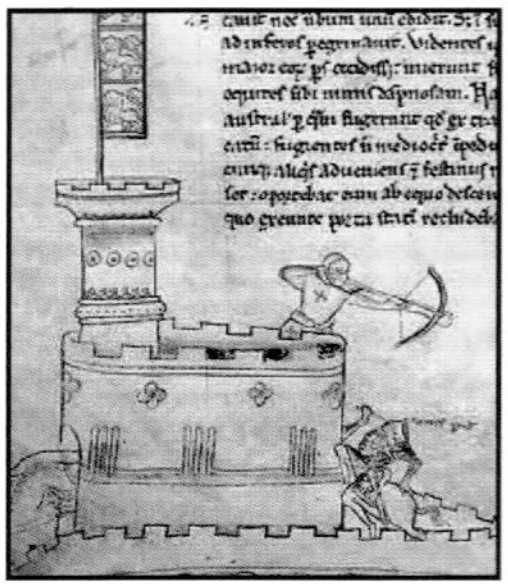

This 13th-century drawing shows a hollow keep.

CRUSADER CASTLES

From 1099-1272, knights from Christian lands went on crusades, or holy wars, to reclaim Jerusalem—the site of Jesus Christ's tomb—from Muslim control. Europeans set up their own states in the Holy Land and built new, incredibly strong castles. Only kings or very rich religious military orders could afford them.

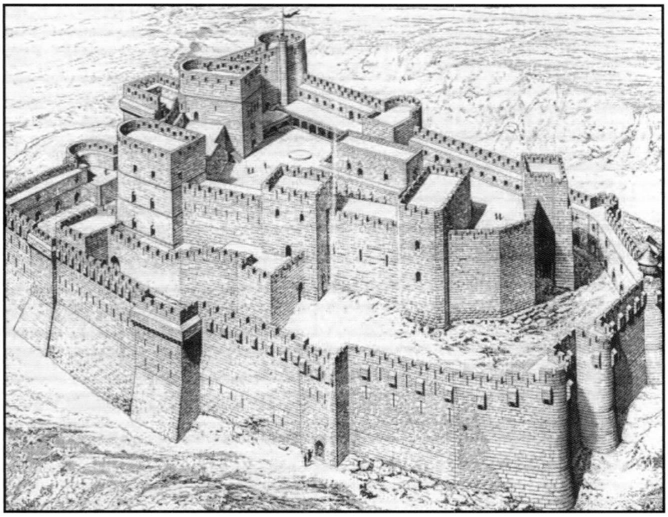

Krak des Chevaliers in Syria was built in 1170 by the wealthy Knights Hospitaller. The castle had concentric lines of defenses, or walls within walls.

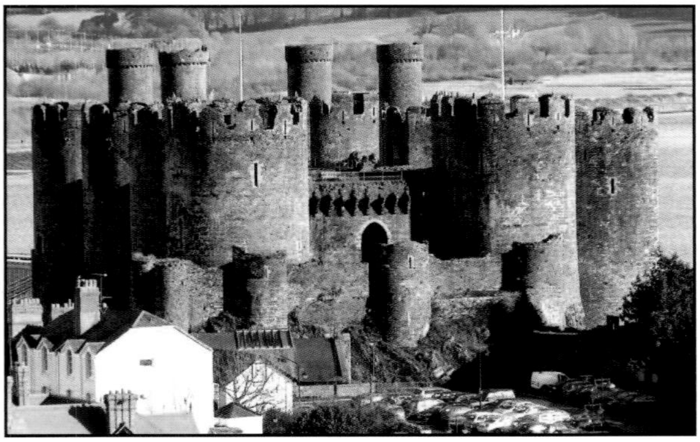

Conwy Castle in Wales, in Great Britain, has a barbican, or fortified gateway, protecting its west front.

GREAT CASTLES

The 11th, 12th, and 13th centuries were a tumultuous time in Europe. It was also the peak of great castle building. New features appeared such as battlements (the jagged tops of castle walls), barbicans (strong gateways), arrow slits in walls for archers to safely shoot, murder holes (holes in the ceiling for ambushing attackers), and machicolations (openings in the floor over a wall). King Henry II's fortress at Dover (see page 20) and the Welsh castles of Edward I (see page 36) helped secure the future of England.

A fortified wall of Carcassonne in France shows the wooden galleries, or machicolations, that were built on most medieval castles.

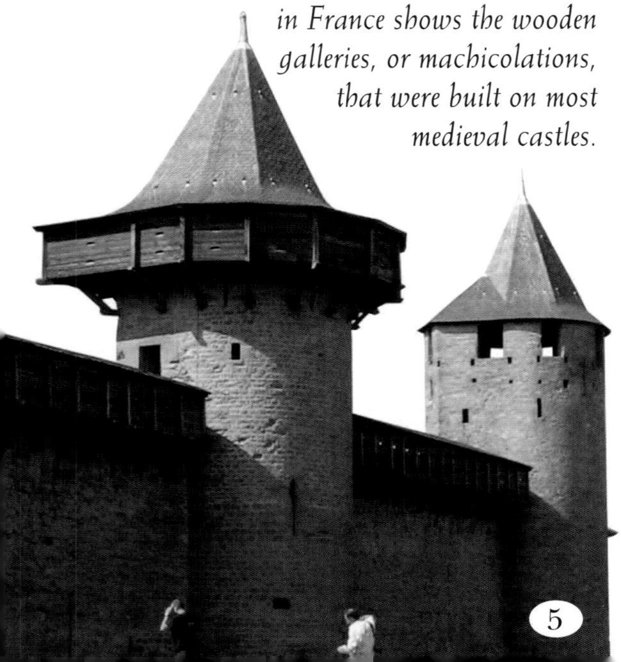

Under Siege!

A 15th-century painting of a siege shows ladders for scaling walls and a large defending army.

A hostile foreign force has invaded. The nobles and their army retreat to the safety of a castle. The invaders arrive and set up camp, then begin the slow and dangerous process of trying to break into the fortress.

A siege engine

Moveable siege towers

CASTLE ATTACK

The besiegers build "engines" out of wood that hurl rocks against the castle walls. They erect towers as firing platforms that can also be pushed against the battlements so that troops can storm the tops of the walls. Sappers dig at the foundations of castle walls to unbalance and topple stone towers. Heavy battering rams are forced against weak points, and flaming arrows are fired into wooden structures on or inside the castle. If this fails, attackers hope to starve the defenders out, before help comes.

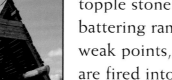

A shielded battering ram

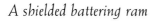

Undermining a castle tower

CASTLE DEFENSE

Defenders have fewer options than attackers. Their best weapons include the crossbow—a good long-range weapon—and boiling oil, which can be poured onto attackers. If needed, a well-stocked castle with its own well can last out for months.

Chateau Gaillard was a strong, highly advanced English castle built in 1196 to defend Normandy, which at that time was a duchy of the English Crown. (See page 8.)

GREAT CASTLE SIEGES

In 1215, rebellious nobles challenged England's King John and took control of Rochester Castle. John himself laid siege to the fortress and, after his catapults failed, he undermined the walls. The nobles and their men retreated to the castle's massive stone keep. John sent men to dig beneath a corner tower. They

The strategically important site of Rochester Castle in Kent, England, was besieged three times between 1088 and 1264. The last siege was relieved by Prince Edward (later King Edward I).

lit pig fat to burn the mine's supports away, and toppled the tower. The traitors retreated further behind a strong inner wall. They still controlled half the building, but, after a few weeks, they were starved out—proof that even the strongest castle could be taken eventually.

The longest siege in medieval England took place 60 years later when forces loyal to Henry III attacked a group of defiant nobles holed up in Kenilworth Castle, in Warwickshire, England. Deadly missiles were hurled at the walls, but a flooded, three-sided moat kept the attackers out until the defenders ran out of food six months later.

The imposing ruins of Kenilworth Castle still stand. The castle resisted an epic siege in 1266, during a period of English civil war.

The Breaking of Chateau Gaillard

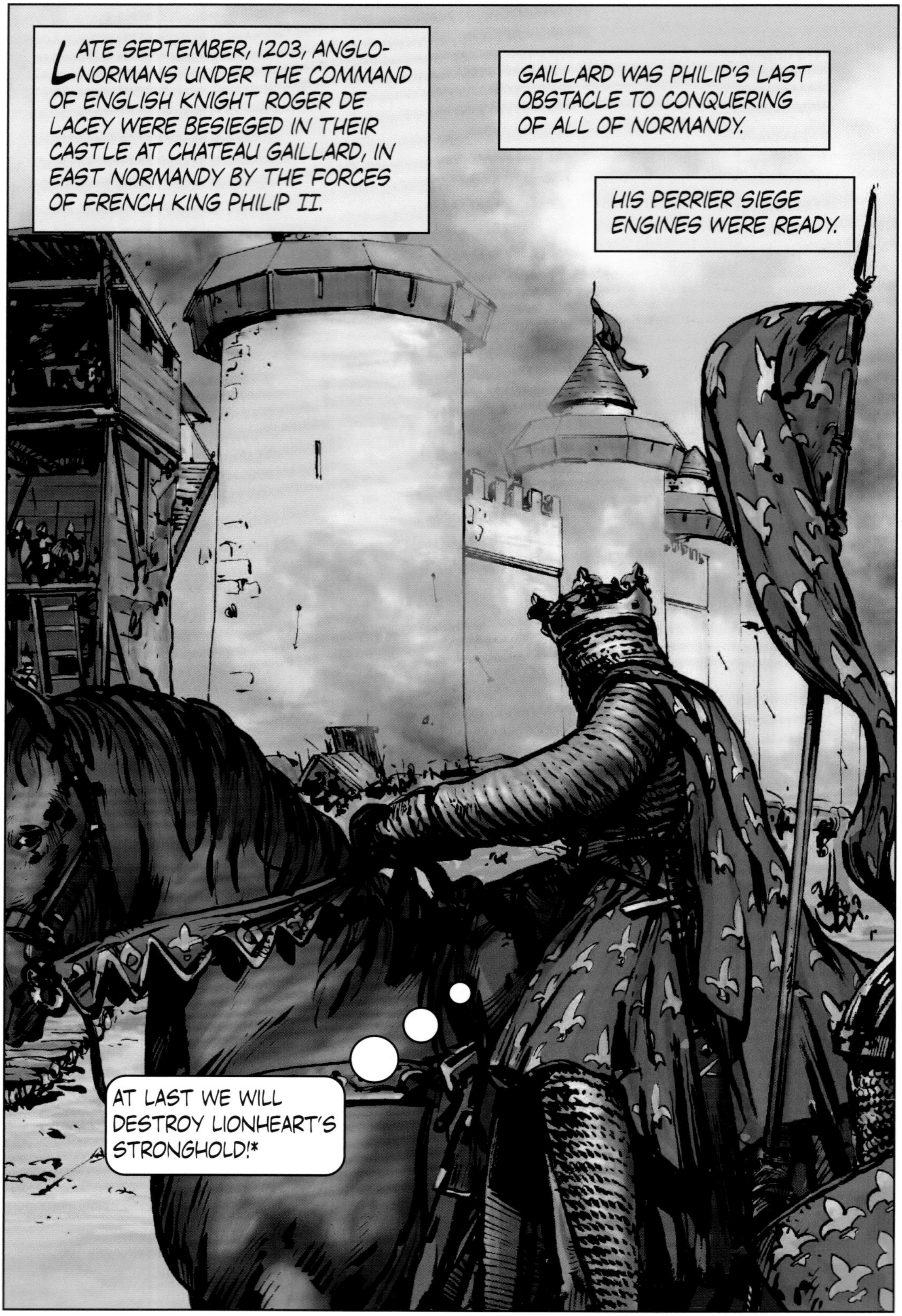
LATE SEPTEMBER, 1203, ANGLO-NORMANS UNDER THE COMMAND OF ENGLISH KNIGHT ROGER DE LACEY WERE BESIEGED IN THEIR CASTLE AT CHATEAU GAILLARD, IN EAST NORMANDY BY THE FORCES OF FRENCH KING PHILIP II.
GAILLARD WAS PHILIP'S LAST OBSTACLE TO CONQUERING OF ALL OF NORMANDY.
HIS PERRIER SIEGE ENGINES WERE READY.
AT LAST WE WILL DESTROY LIONHEART'S STRONGHOLD!*

*ENGLISH KING RICHARD I, KNOWN AS LIONHEART, HAD BUILT GAILLARD.

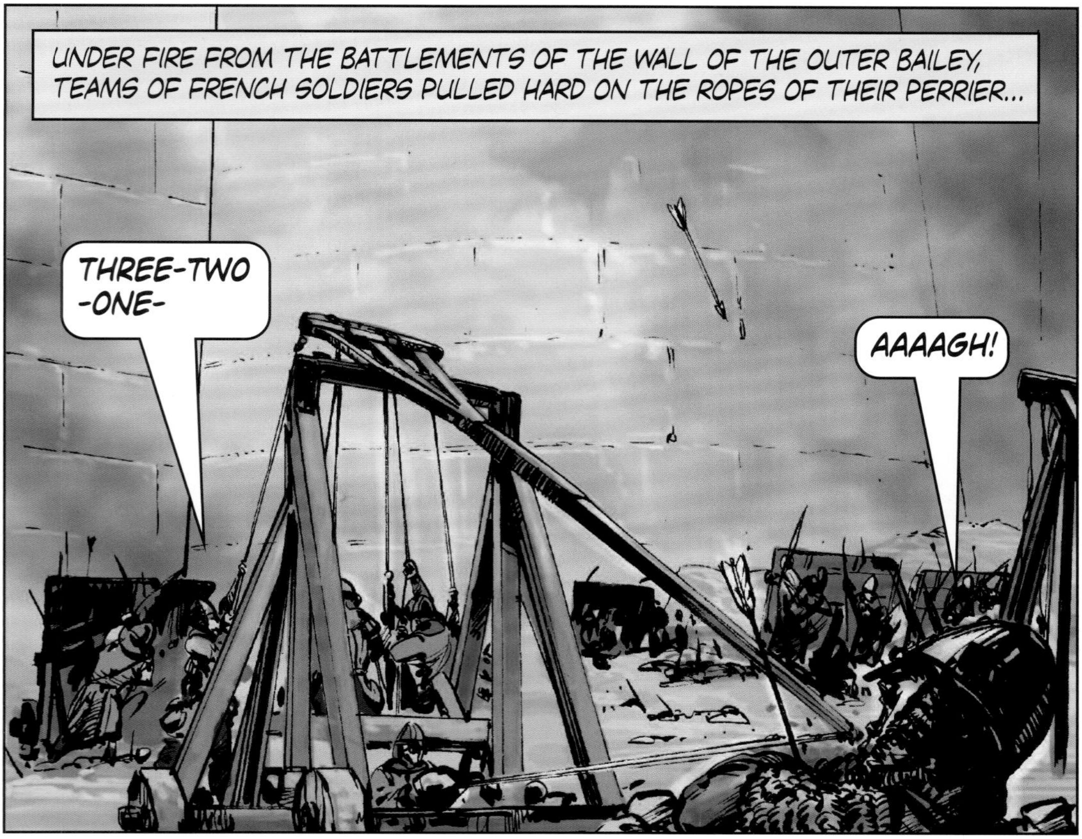
UNDER FIRE FROM THE BATTLEMENTS OF THE WALL OF THE OUTER BAILEY, TEAMS OF FRENCH SOLDIERS PULLED HARD ON THE ROPES OF THEIR PERRIER...
THREE-TWO -ONE-
AAAAGH!

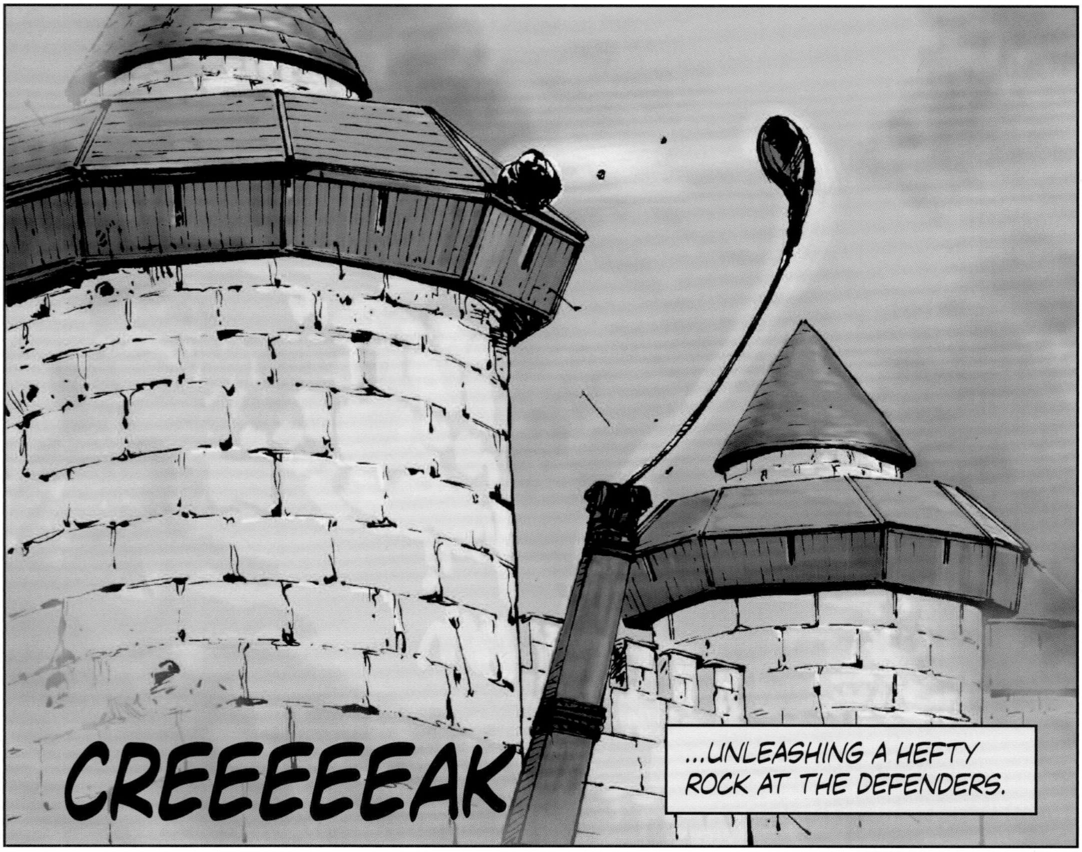
CREEEEEAK
...UNLEASHING A HEFTY ROCK AT THE DEFENDERS.

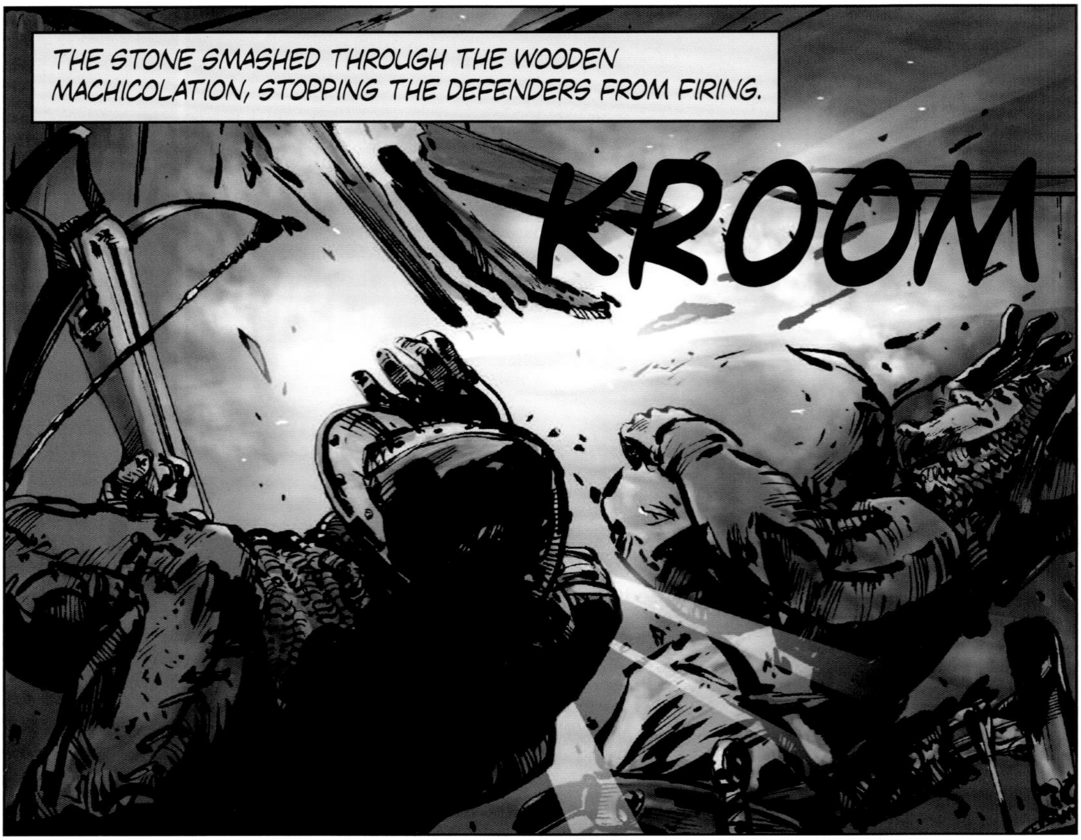
THE STONE SMASHED THROUGH THE WOODEN MACHICOLATION, STOPPING THE DEFENDERS FROM FIRING.
KROOM

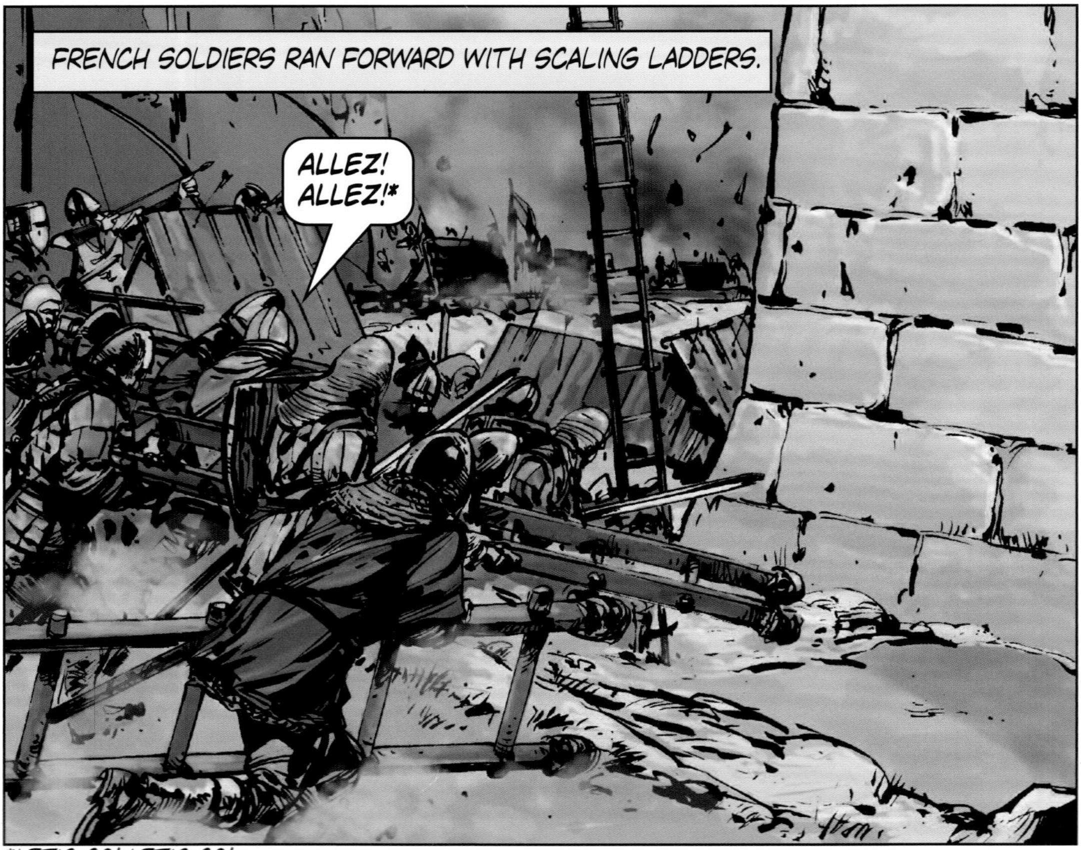
FRENCH SOLDIERS RAN FORWARD WITH SCALING LADDERS.
ALLEZ! ALLEZ!*

*LET'S GO! LET'S GO!

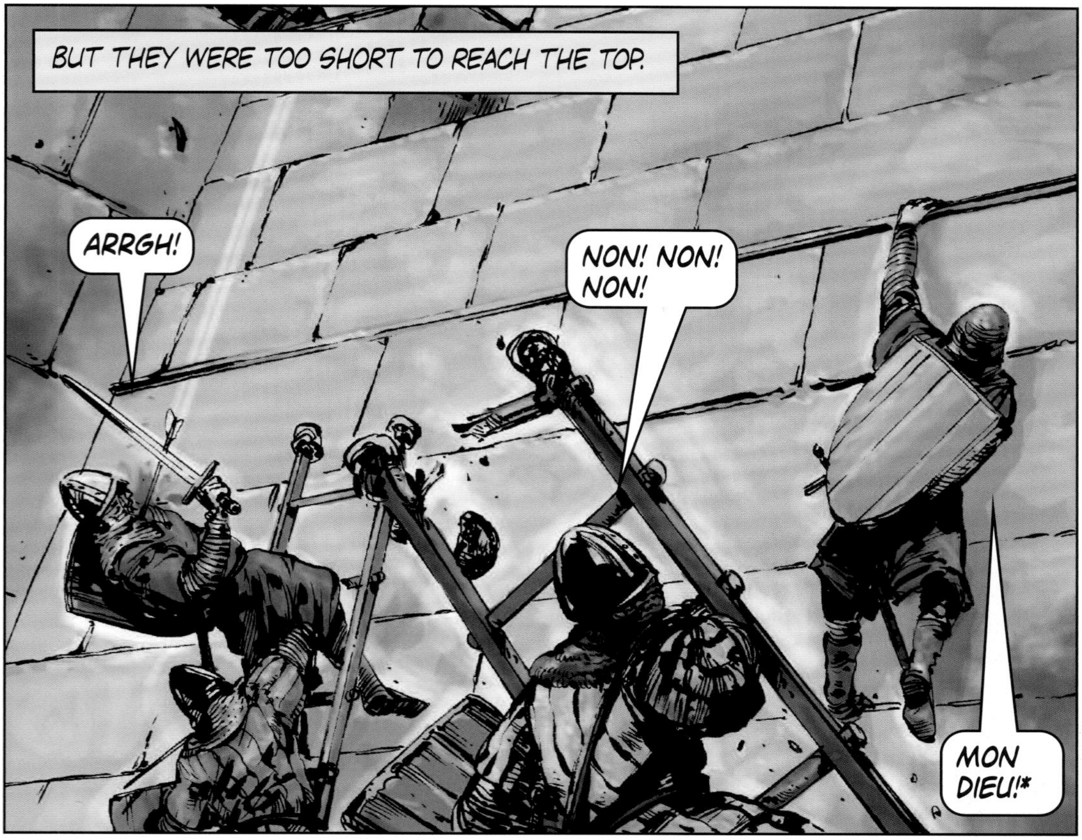
BUT THEY WERE TOO SHORT TO REACH THE TOP.
ARRGH!
NON! NON! NON!
MON DIEU!*

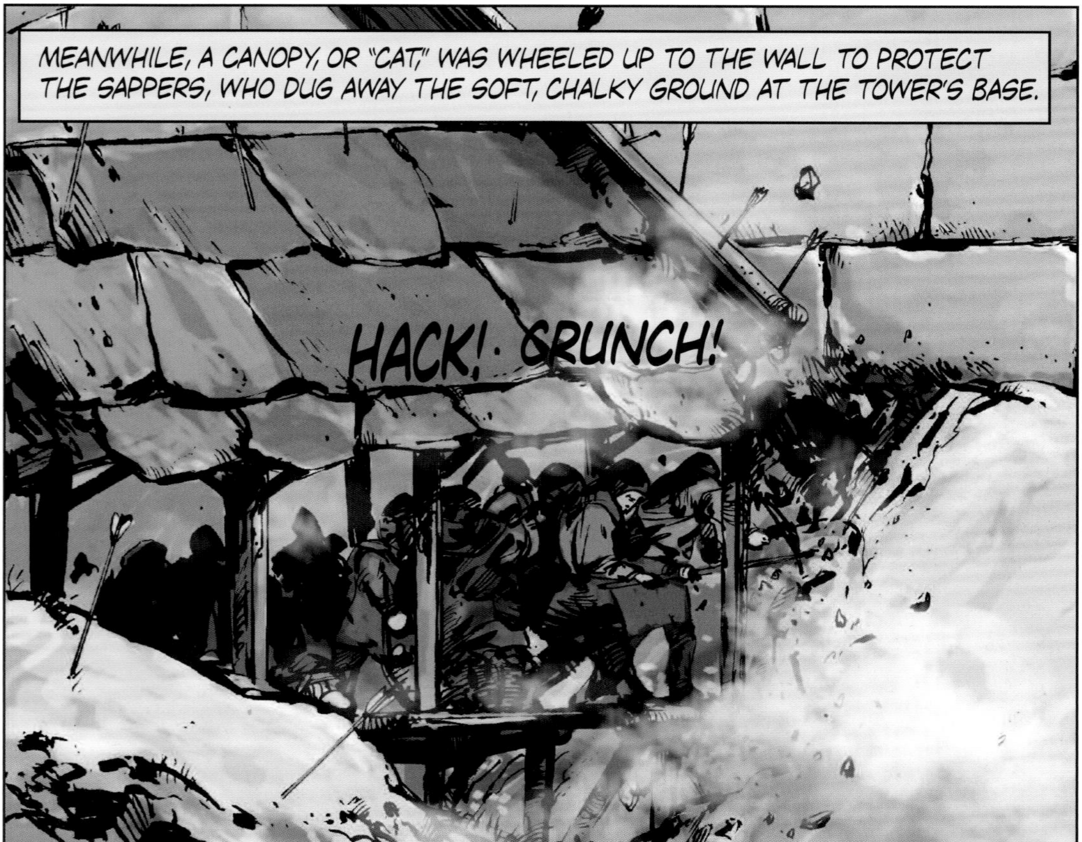
MEANWHILE, A CANOPY, OR "CAT," WAS WHEELED UP TO THE WALL TO PROTECT THE SAPPERS, WHO DUG AWAY THE SOFT, CHALKY GROUND AT THE TOWER'S BASE.
HACK! CRUNCH!

*MY GOD!

SUDDENLY, WITH AN EARTHSHAKING RUMBLE, THE OUTER STONES OF THE TOWER COLLAPSED, TAKING THE WOODEN STRUCTURES WITH THEM.

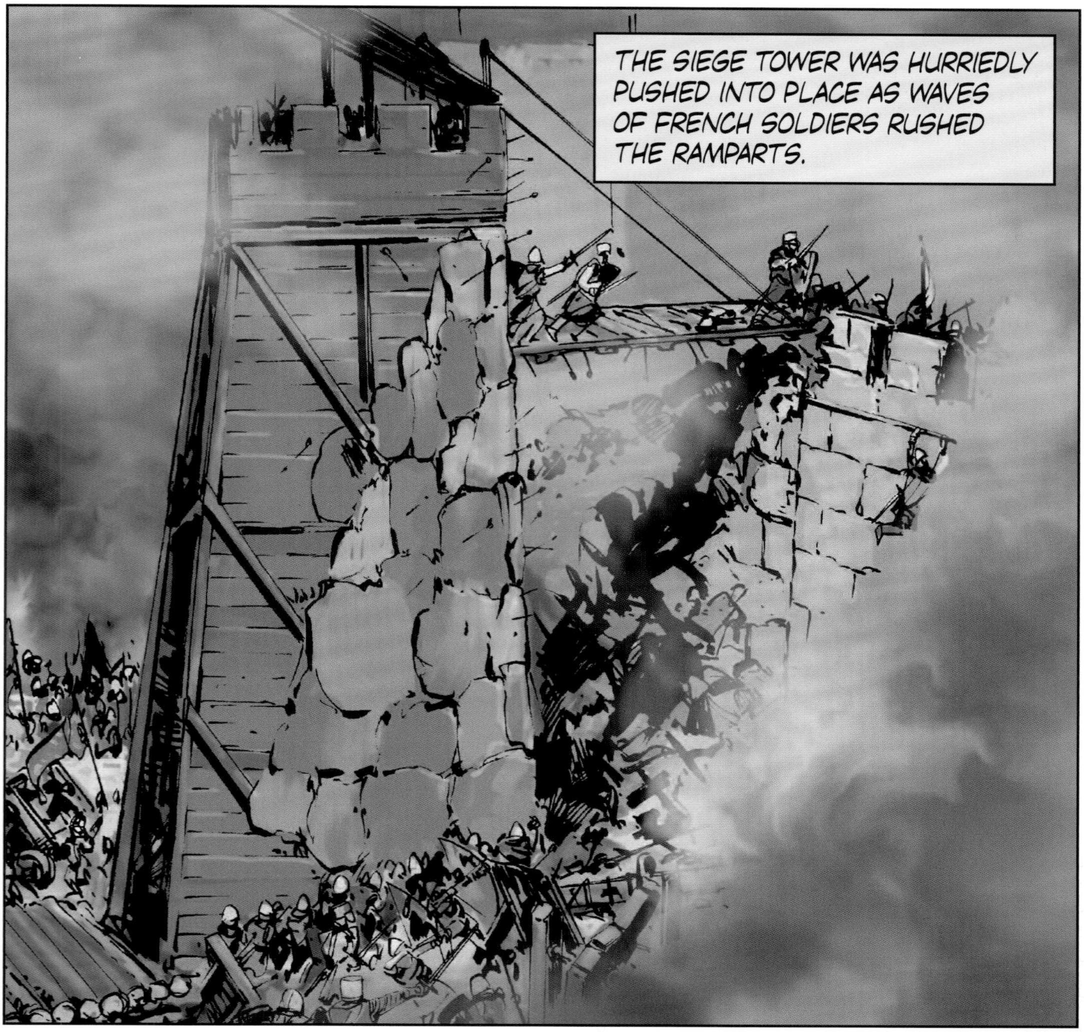
THE SIEGE TOWER WAS HURRIEDLY PUSHED INTO PLACE AS WAVES OF FRENCH SOLDIERS RUSHED THE RAMPARTS.

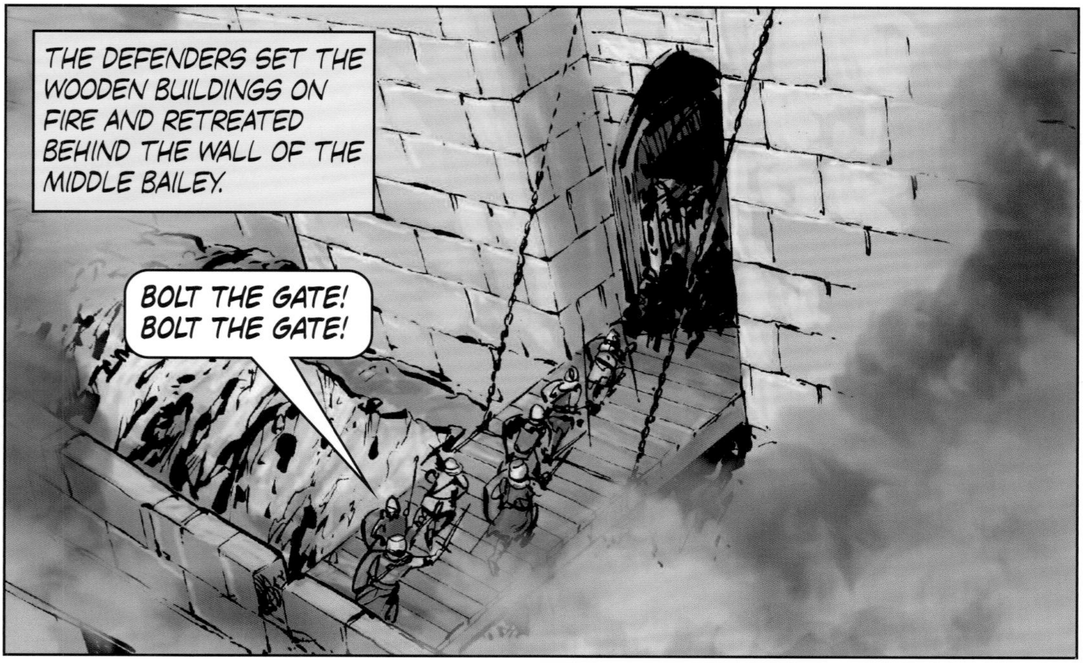
THE DEFENDERS SET THE WOODEN BUILDINGS ON FIRE AND RETREATED BEHIND THE WALL OF THE MIDDLE BAILEY.
BOLT THE GATE! BOLT THE GATE!

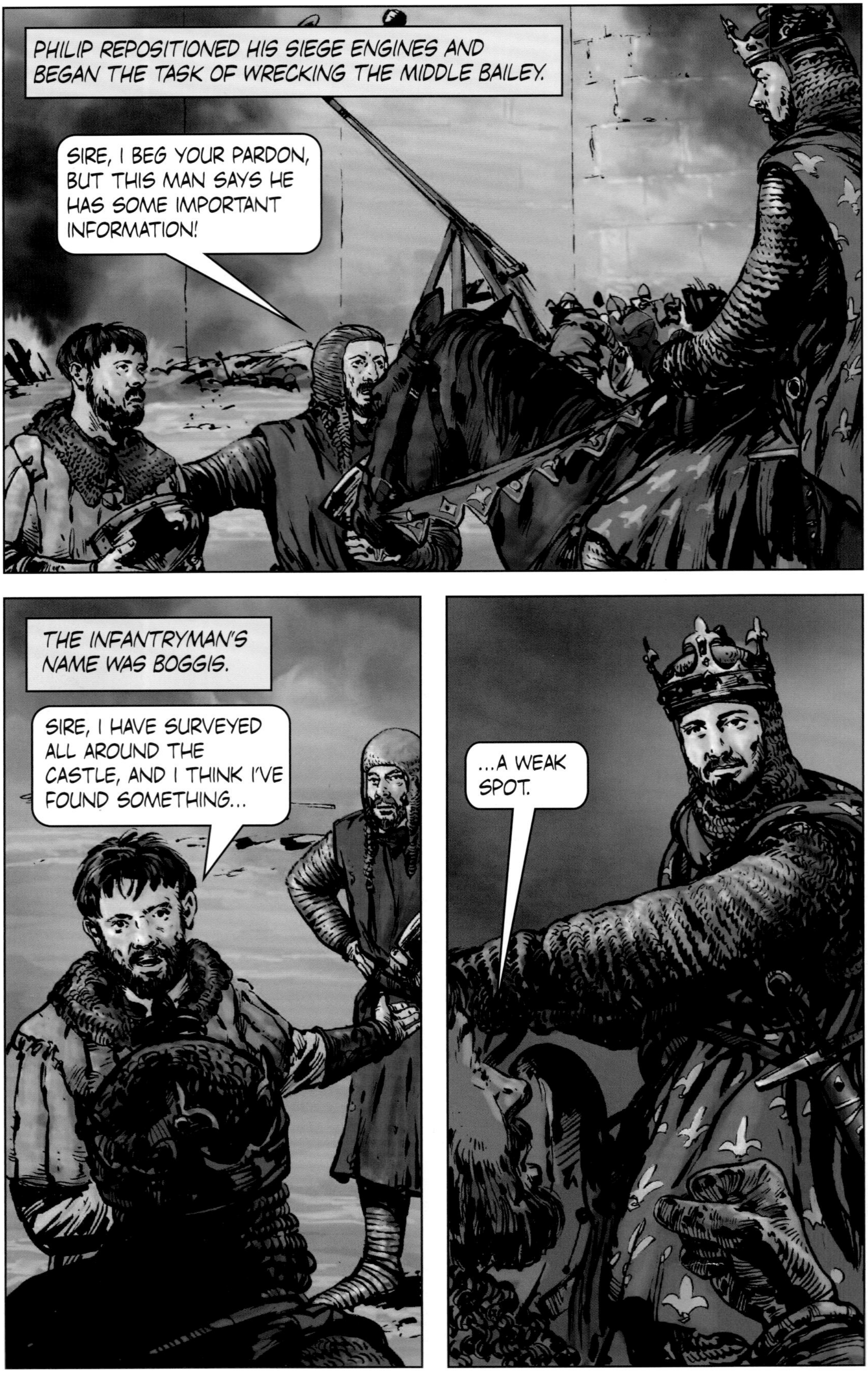
PHILIP REPOSITIONED HIS SIEGE ENGINES AND BEGAN THE TASK OF WRECKING THE MIDDLE BAILEY.
SIRE, I BEG YOUR PARDON, BUT THIS MAN SAYS HE HAS SOME IMPORTANT INFORMATION!
THE INFANTRYMAN'S NAME WAS BOGGIS.
SIRE, I HAVE SURVEYED ALL AROUND THE CASTLE, AND I THINK I'VE FOUND SOMETHING...
...A WEAK SPOT.

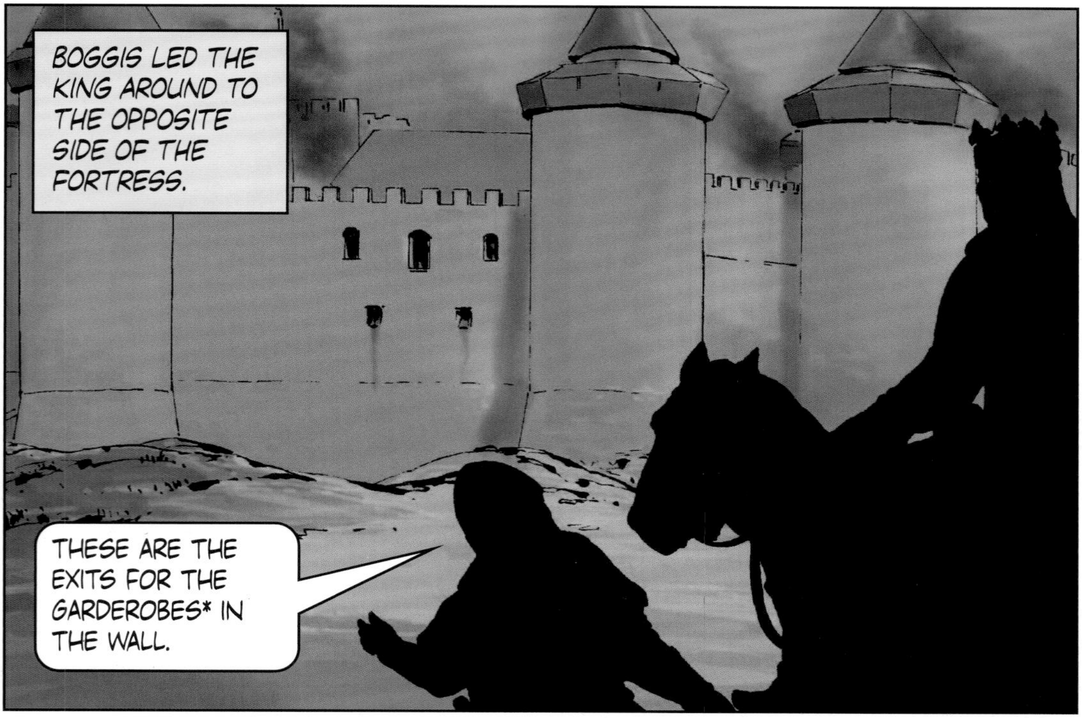
BOGGIS LED THE KING AROUND TO THE OPPOSITE SIDE OF THE FORTRESS.
THESE ARE THE EXITS FOR THE GARDEROBES* IN THE WALL.

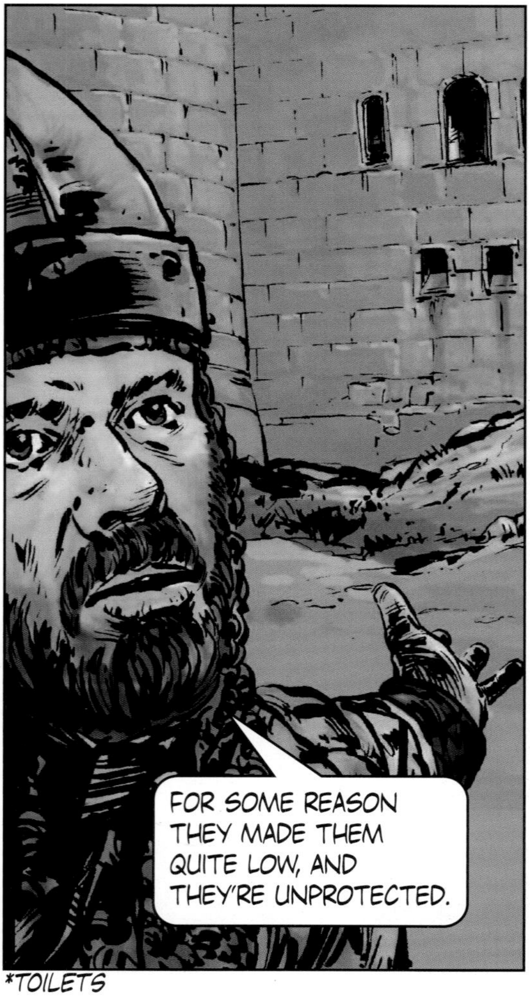
FOR SOME REASON THEY MADE THEM QUITE LOW, AND THEY'RE UNPROTECTED.

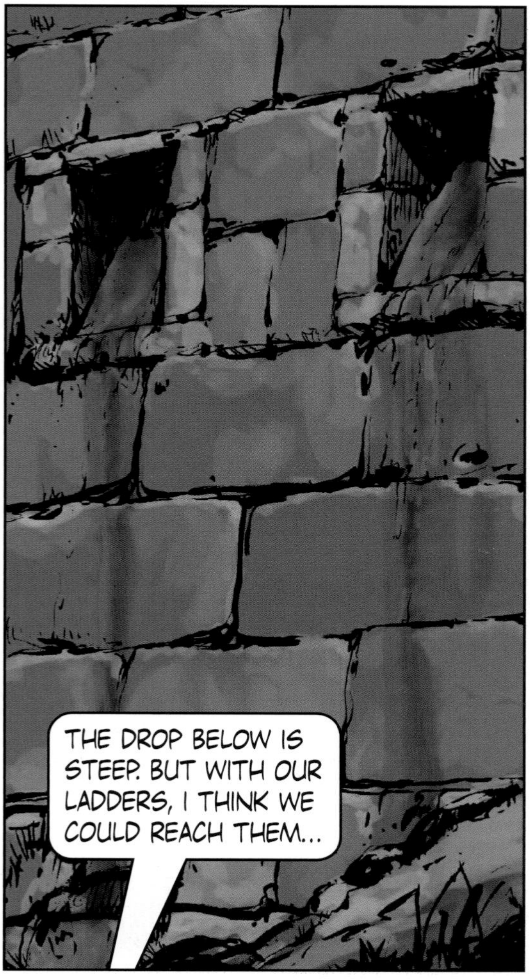
THE DROP BELOW IS STEEP. BUT WITH OUR LADDERS, I THINK WE COULD REACH THEM...

*TOILETS

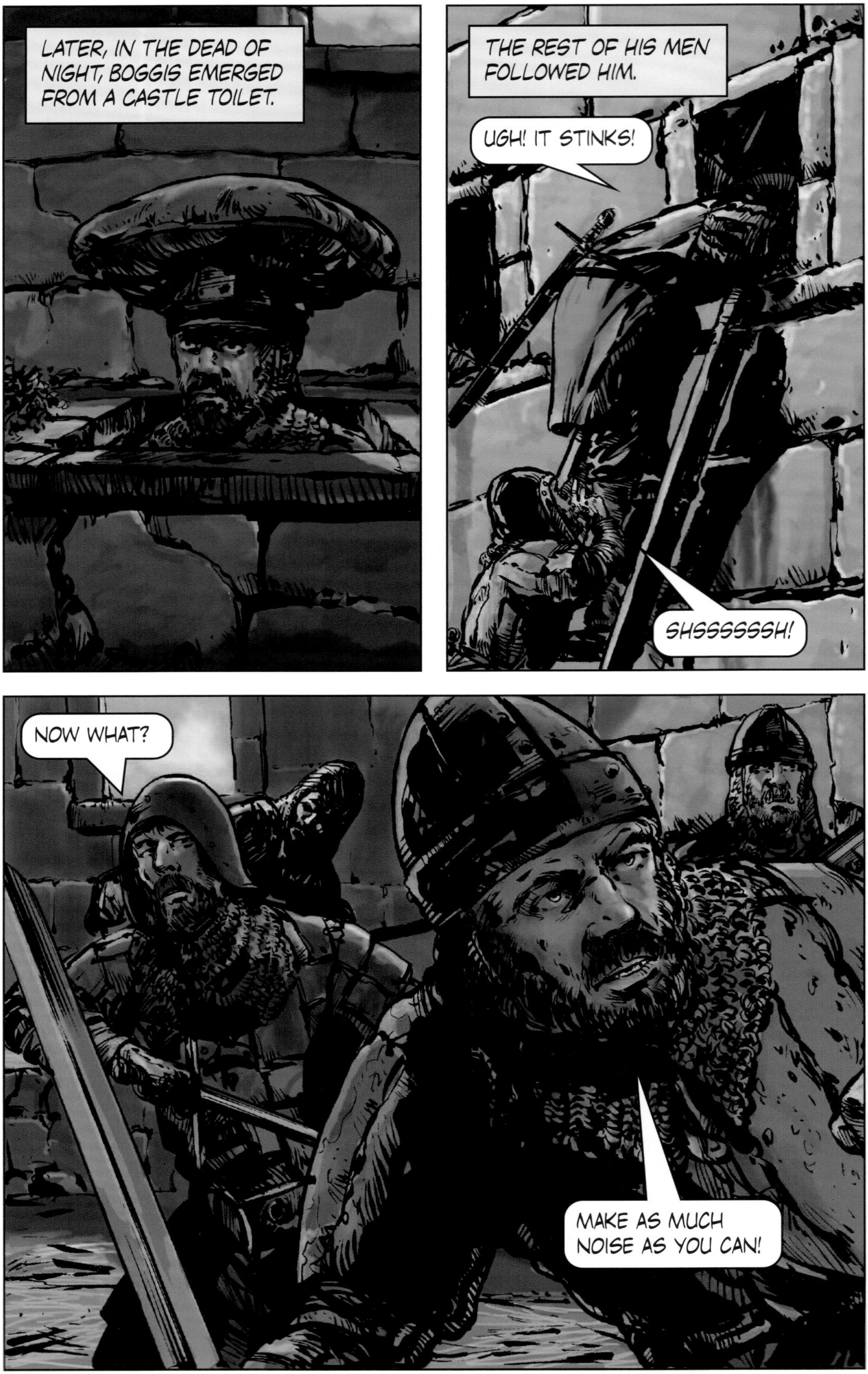
LATER, IN THE DEAD OF NIGHT, BOGGIS EMERGED FROM A CASTLE TOILET.
THE REST OF HIS MEN FOLLOWED HIM.
UGH! IT STINKS!
SHSSSSSSH!
NOW WHAT?
MAKE AS MUCH NOISE AS YOU CAN!

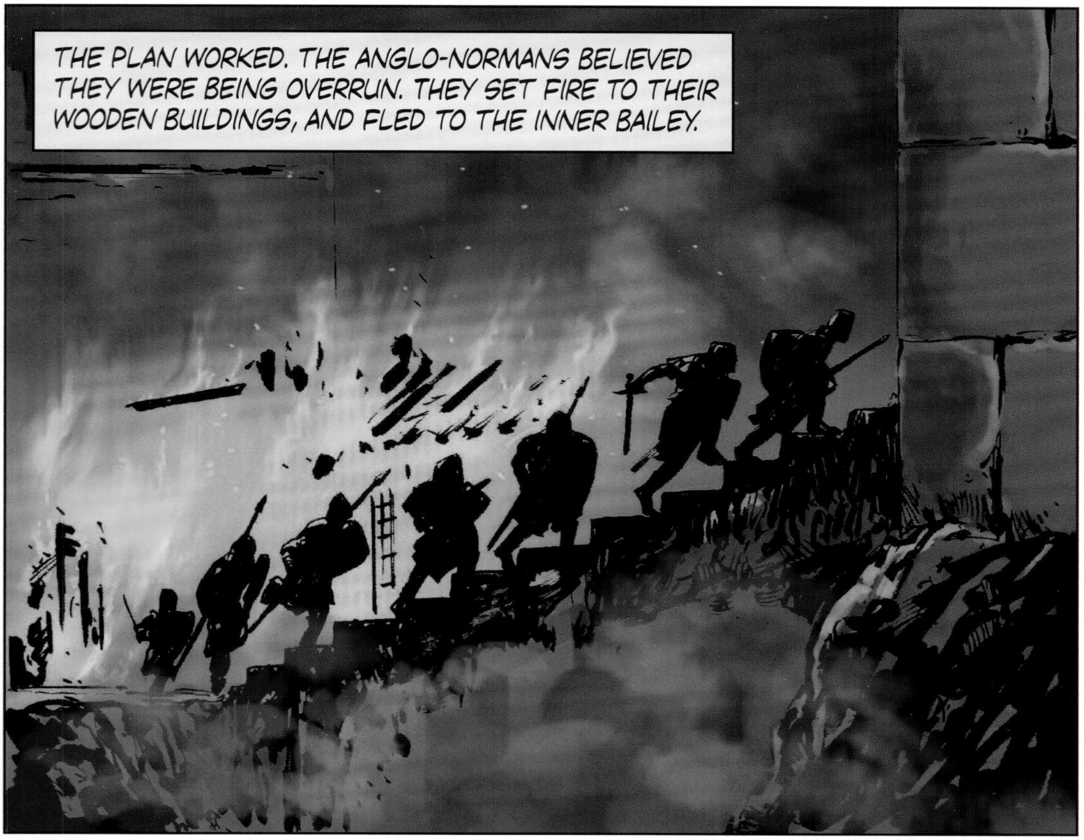
THE PLAN WORKED. THE ANGLO-NORMANS BELIEVED THEY WERE BEING OVERRUN. THEY SET FIRE TO THEIR WOODEN BUILDINGS, AND FLED TO THE INNER BAILEY.

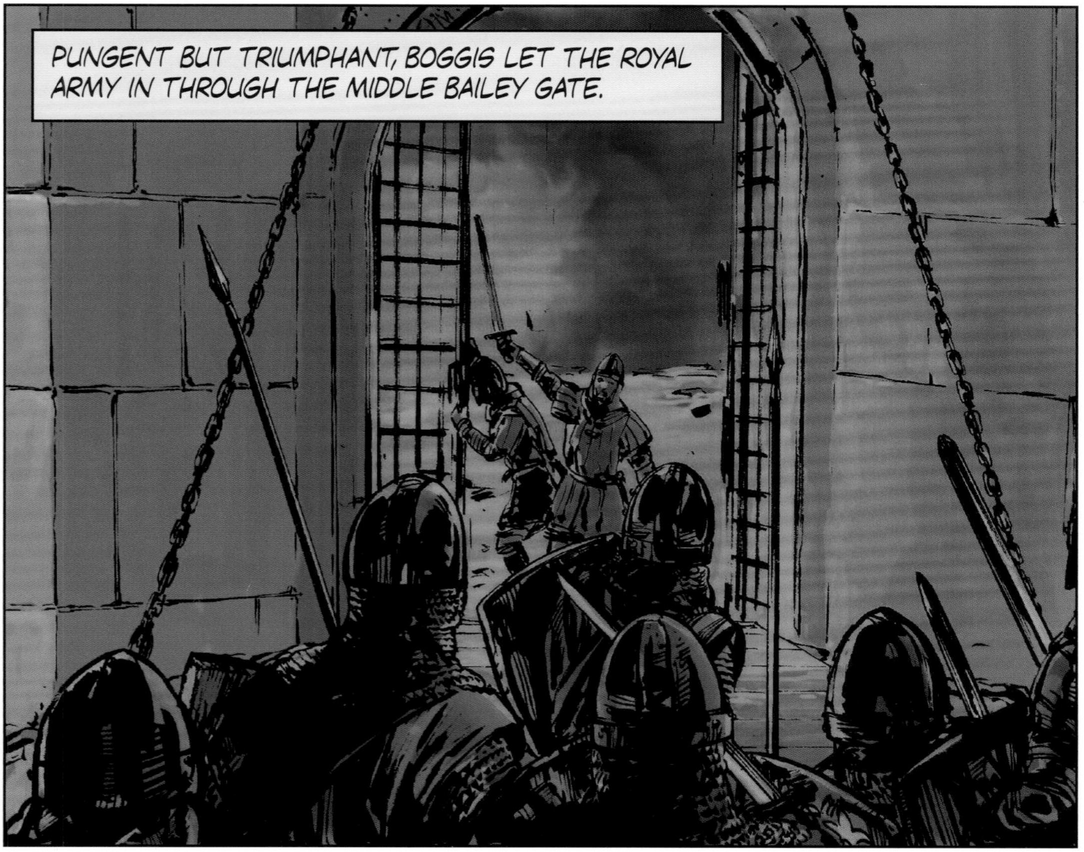
PUNGENT BUT TRIUMPHANT, BOGGIS LET THE ROYAL ARMY IN THROUGH THE MIDDLE BAILEY GATE.

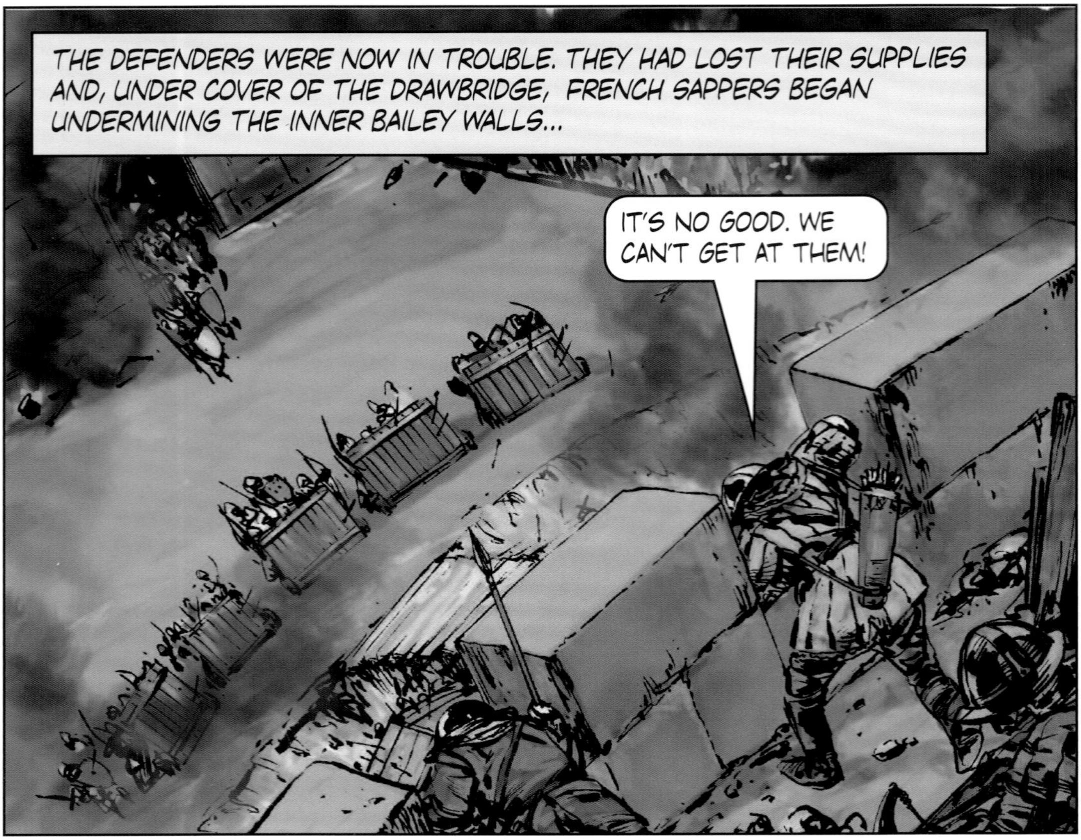
THE DEFENDERS WERE NOW IN TROUBLE. THEY HAD LOST THEIR SUPPLIES AND, UNDER COVER OF THE DRAWBRIDGE, FRENCH SAPPERS BEGAN UNDERMINING THE INNER BAILEY WALLS...
IT'S NO GOOD. WE CAN'T GET AT THEM!

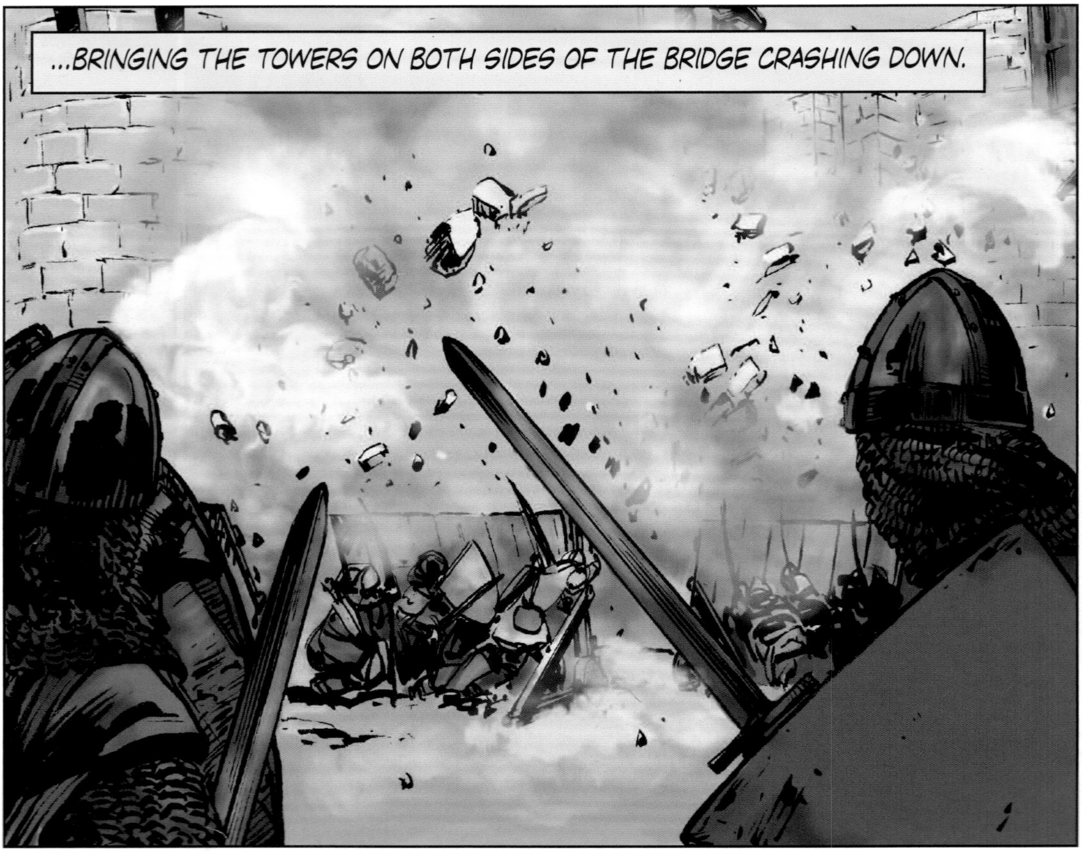
...BRINGING THE TOWERS ON BOTH SIDES OF THE BRIDGE CRASHING DOWN.

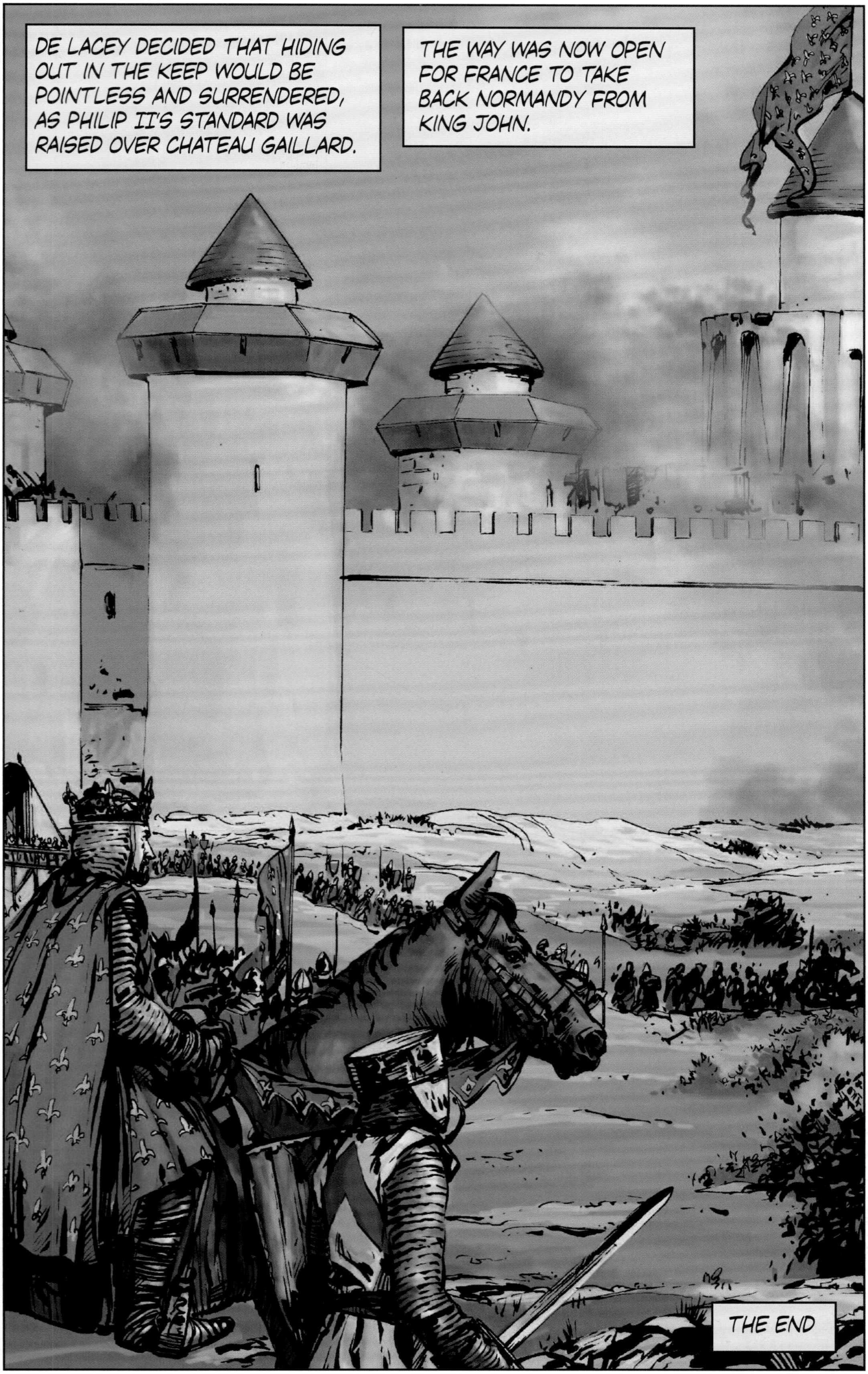
DE LACEY DECIDED THAT HIDING OUT IN THE KEEP WOULD BE POINTLESS AND SURRENDERED, AS PHILIP II'S STANDARD WAS RAISED OVER CHATEAU GAILLARD.
THE WAY WAS NOW OPEN FOR FRANCE TO TAKE BACK NORMANDY FROM KING JOHN.
THE END

The Siege of Dover Castle

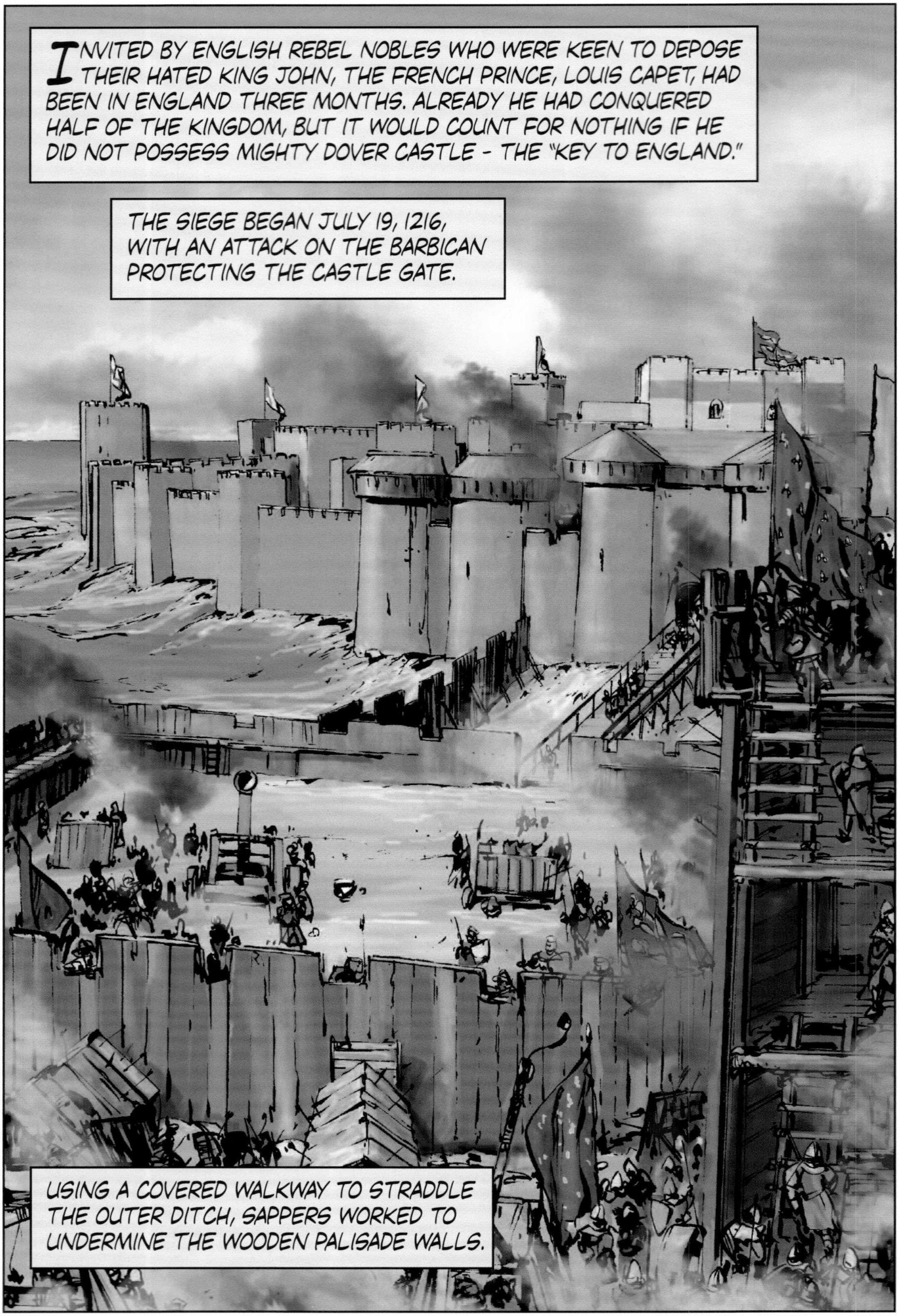
INVITED BY ENGLISH REBEL NOBLES WHO WERE KEEN TO DEPOSE THEIR HATED KING JOHN, THE FRENCH PRINCE, LOUIS CAPET, HAD BEEN IN ENGLAND THREE MONTHS. ALREADY HE HAD CONQUERED HALF OF THE KINGDOM, BUT IT WOULD COUNT FOR NOTHING IF HE DID NOT POSSESS MIGHTY DOVER CASTLE - THE "KEY TO ENGLAND."
THE SIEGE BEGAN JULY 19, 1216, WITH AN ATTACK ON THE BARBICAN PROTECTING THE CASTLE GATE.
USING A COVERED WALKWAY TO STRADDLE THE OUTER DITCH, SAPPERS WORKED TO UNDERMINE THE WOODEN PALISADE WALLS.

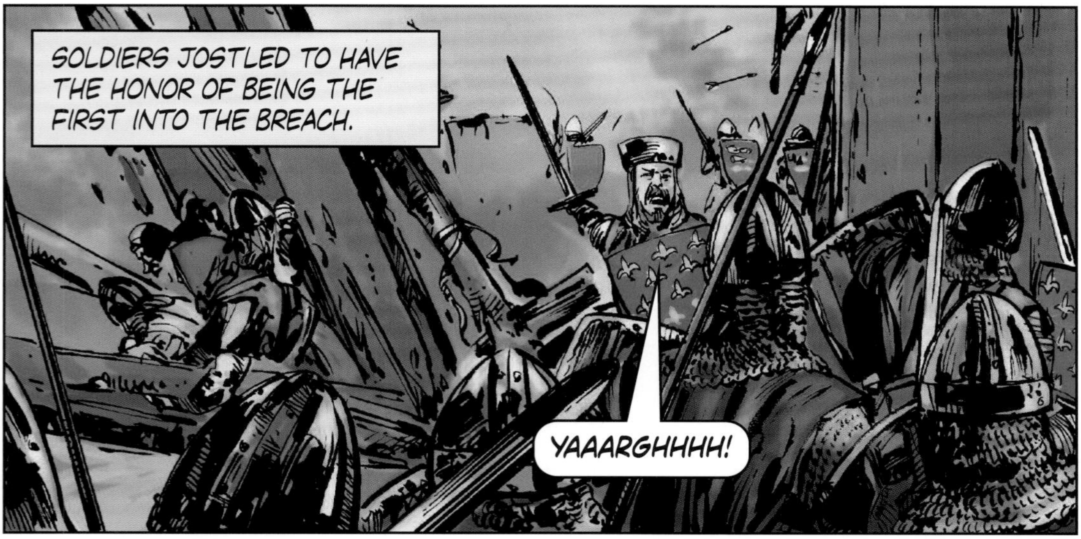
SOLDIERS JOSTLED TO HAVE THE HONOR OF BEING THE FIRST INTO THE BREACH.
YAAARGHHHH!

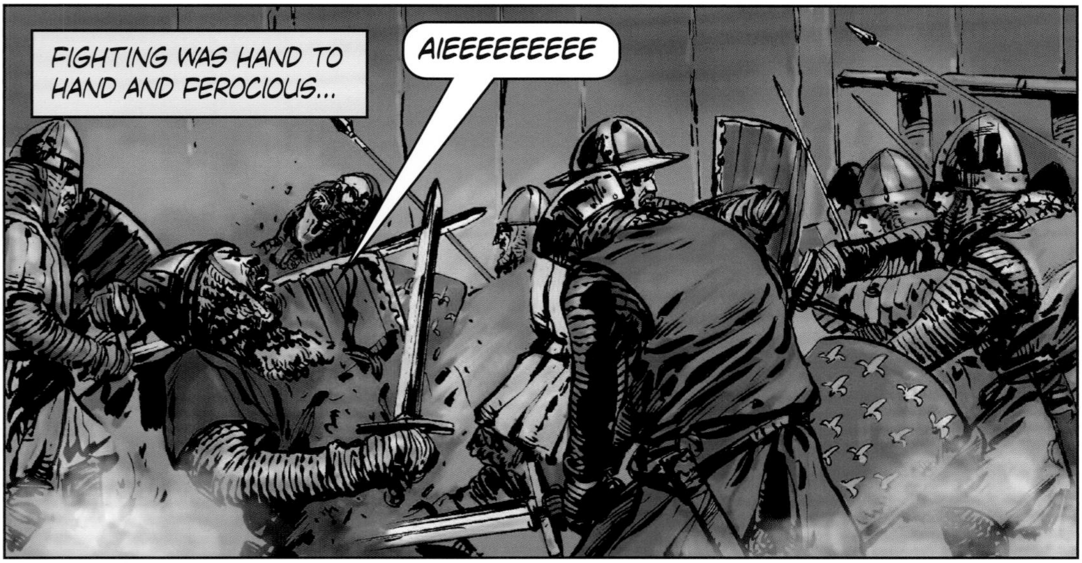
FIGHTING WAS HAND TO HAND AND FEROCIOUS...
AIEEEEEEEEE

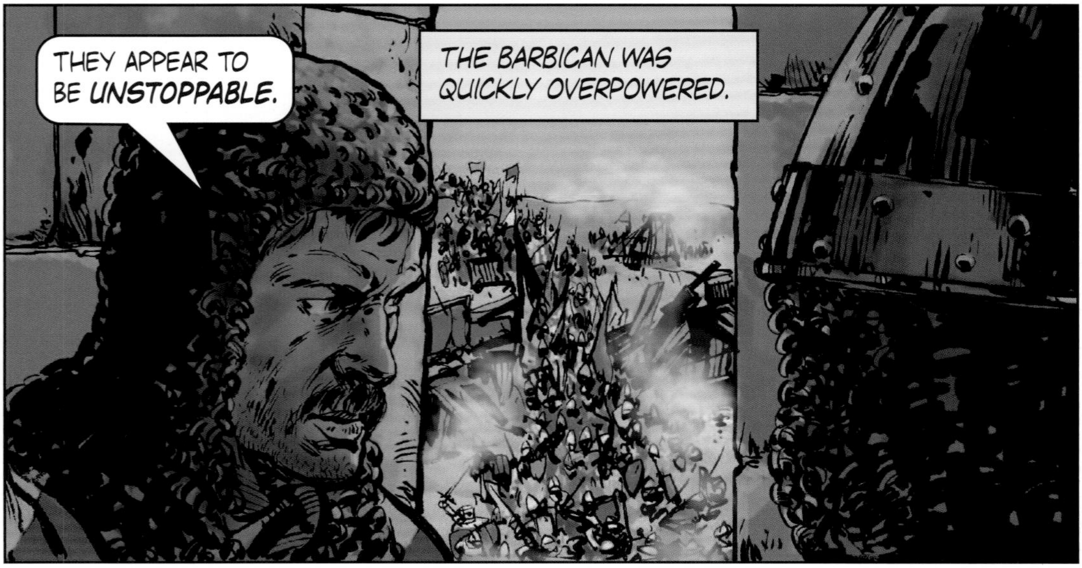
THEY APPEAR TO BE UNSTOPPABLE.
THE BARBICAN WAS QUICKLY OVERPOWERED.

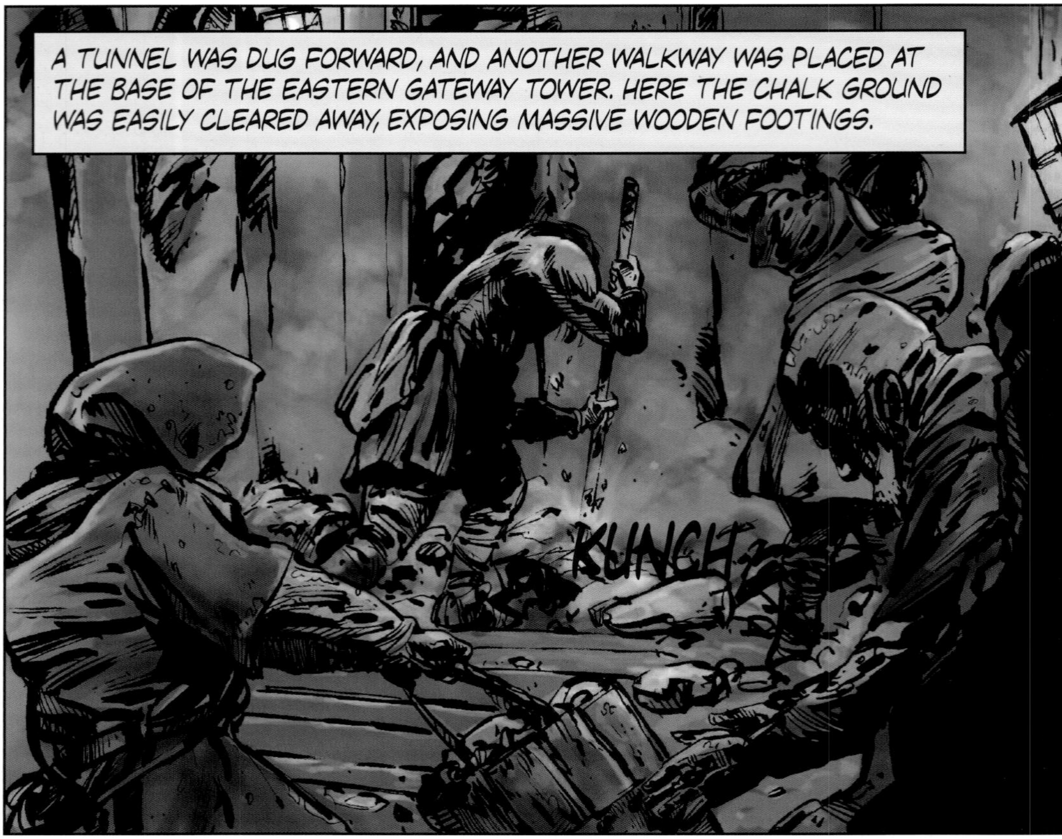
A TUNNEL WAS DUG FORWARD, AND ANOTHER WALKWAY WAS PLACED AT THE BASE OF THE EASTERN GATEWAY TOWER. HERE THE CHALK GROUND WAS EASILY CLEARED AWAY, EXPOSING MASSIVE WOODEN FOOTINGS.
KUNCH

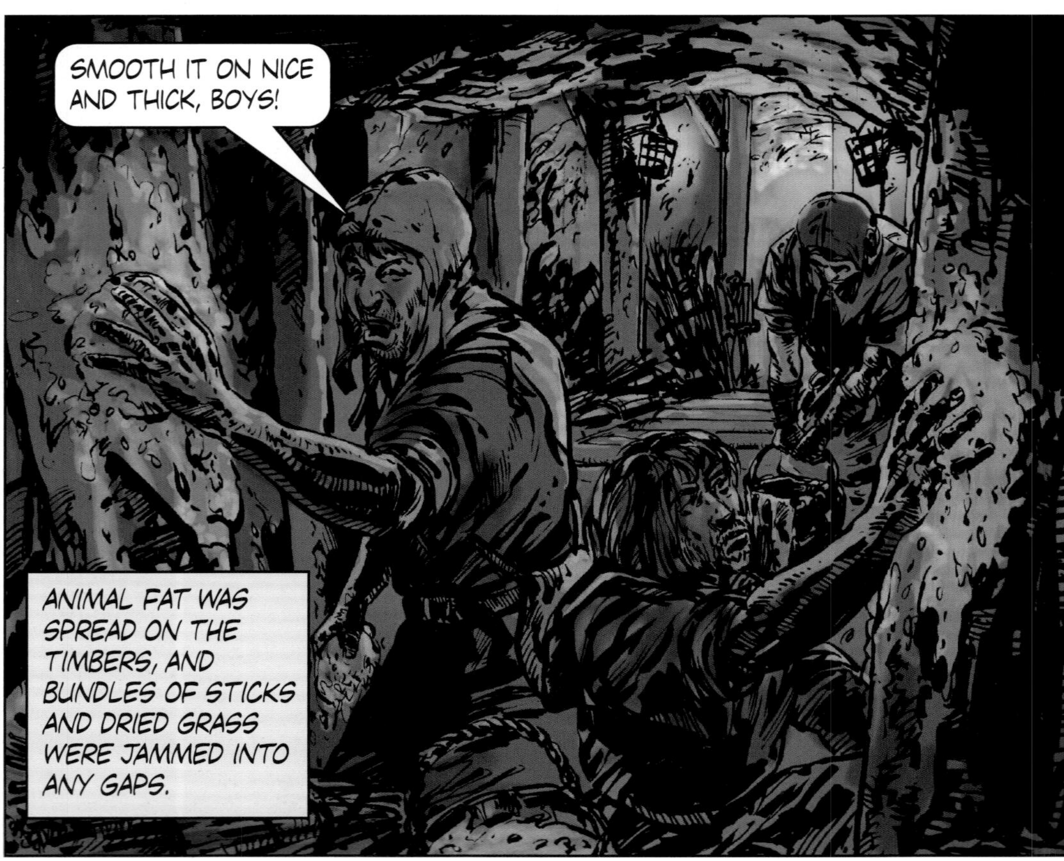
SMOOTH IT ON NICE AND THICK, BOYS!
ANIMAL FAT WAS SPREAD ON THE TIMBERS, AND BUNDLES OF STICKS AND DRIED GRASS WERE JAMMED INTO ANY GAPS.

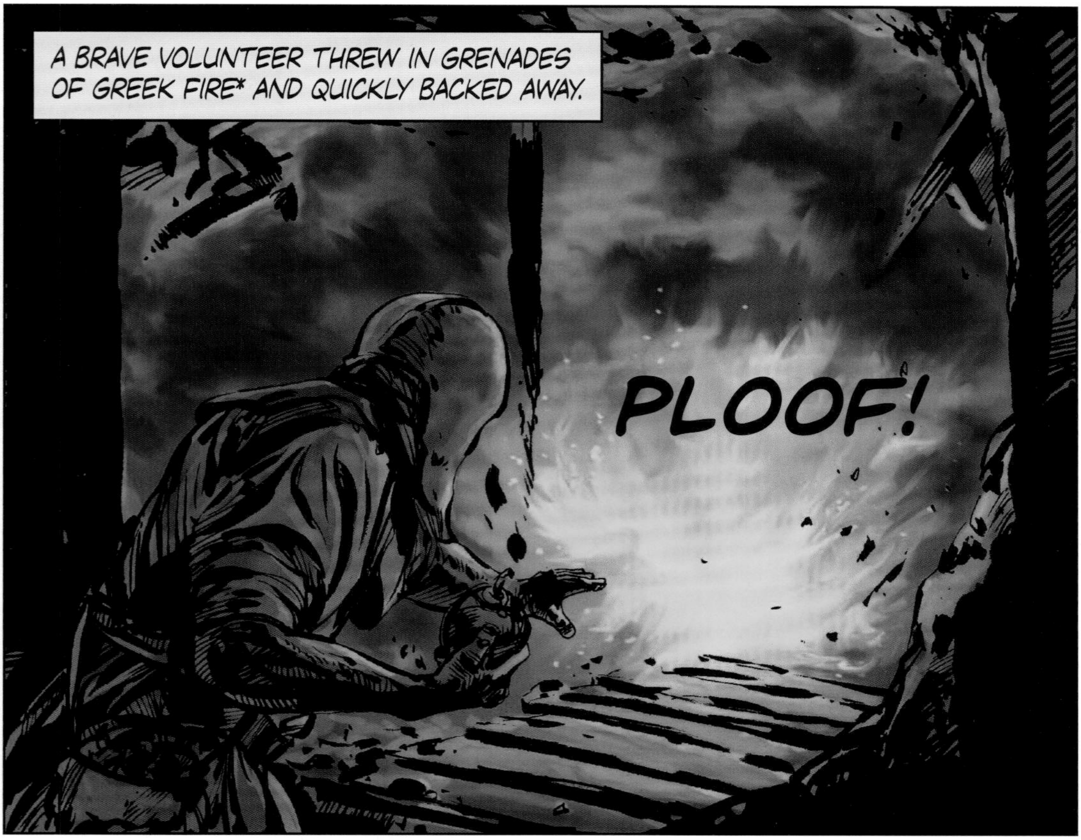
A BRAVE VOLUNTEER THREW IN GRENADES OF GREEK FIRE* AND QUICKLY BACKED AWAY.
PLOOF!

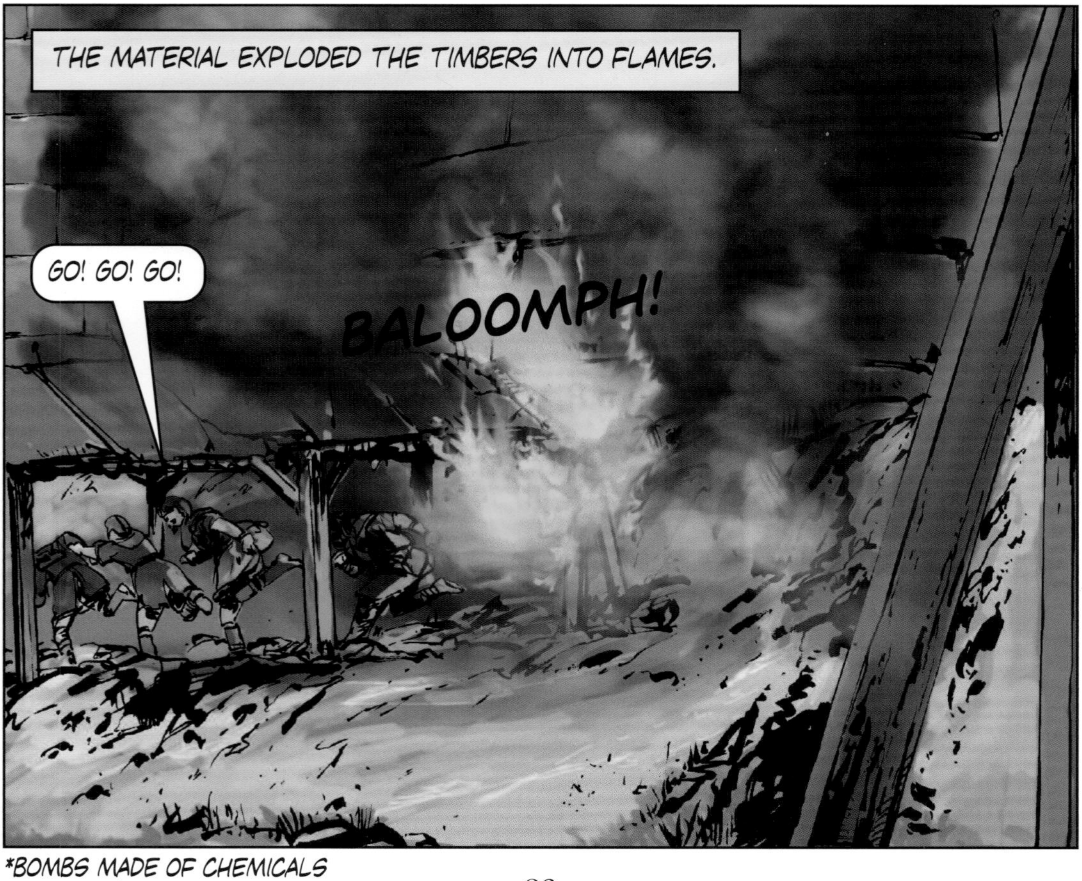
THE MATERIAL EXPLODED THE TIMBERS INTO FLAMES.
GO! GO! GO!
BALOOMPH!

*BOMBS MADE OF CHEMICALS THAT EASILY EXPLODE

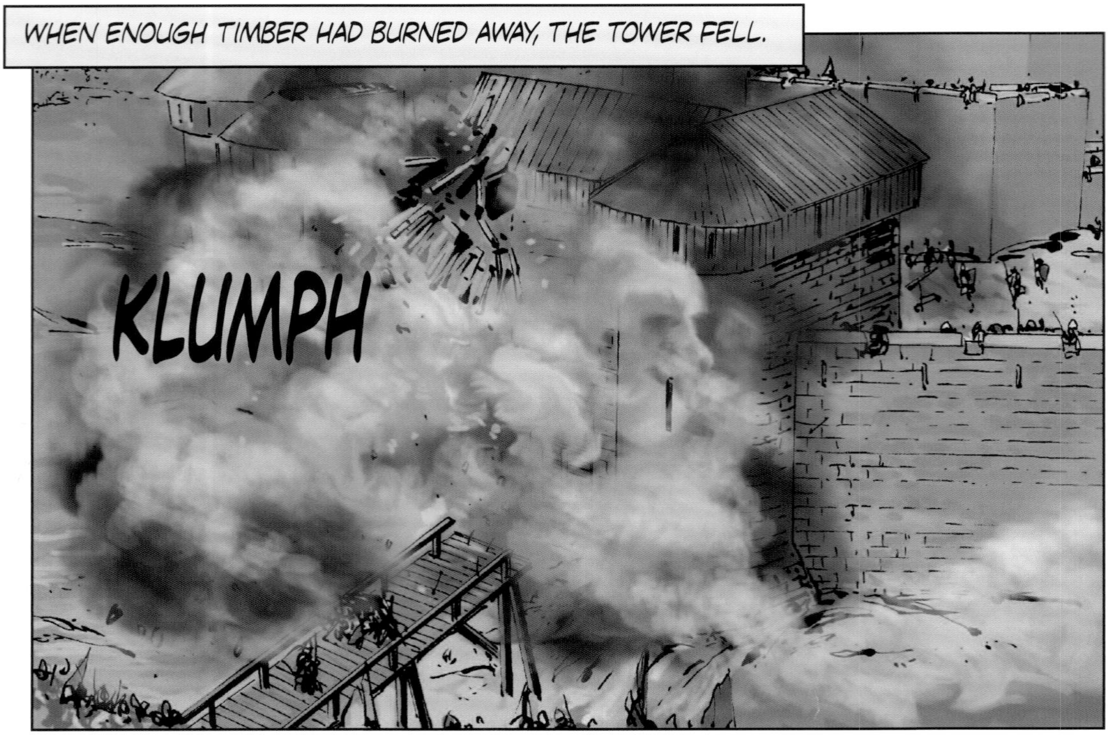
WHEN ENOUGH TIMBER HAD BURNED AWAY, THE TOWER FELL.
KLUMPH

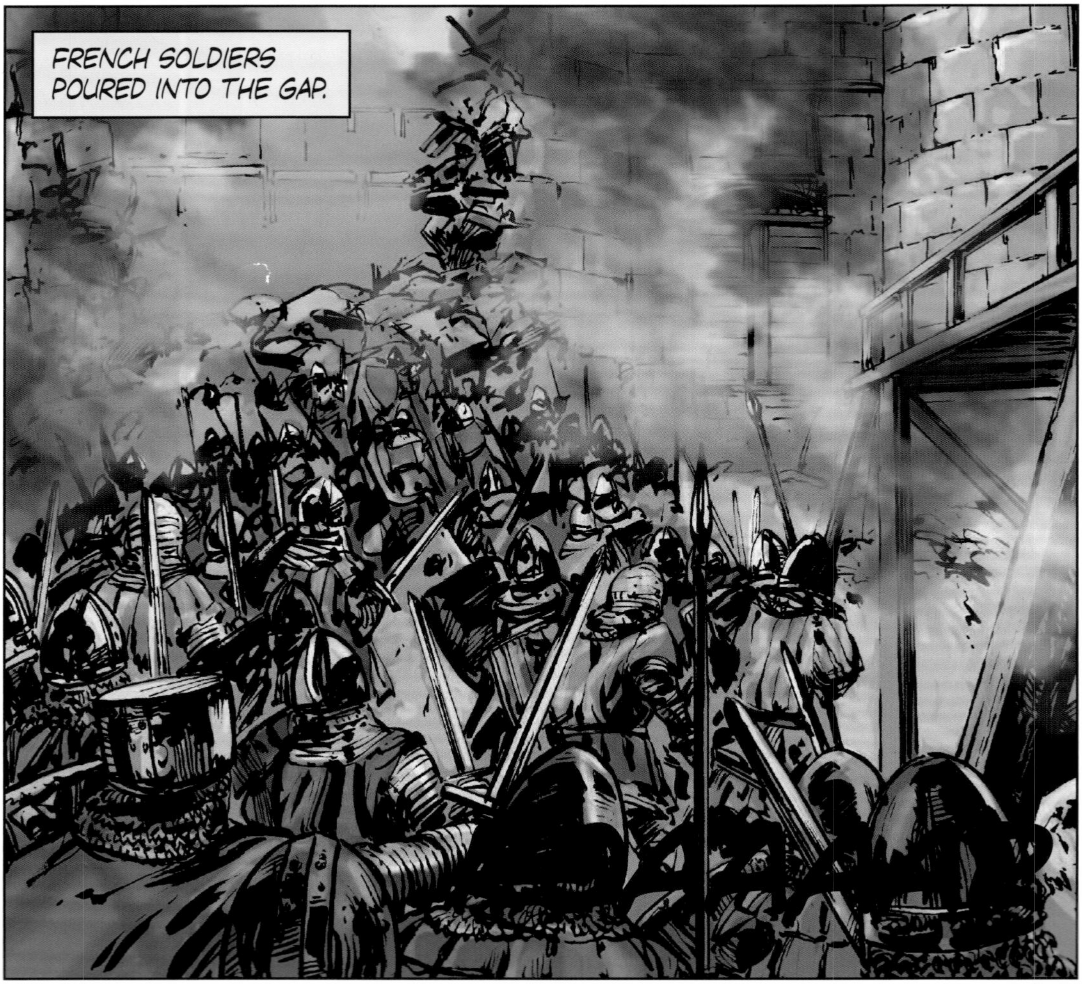
FRENCH SOLDIERS POURED INTO THE GAP.

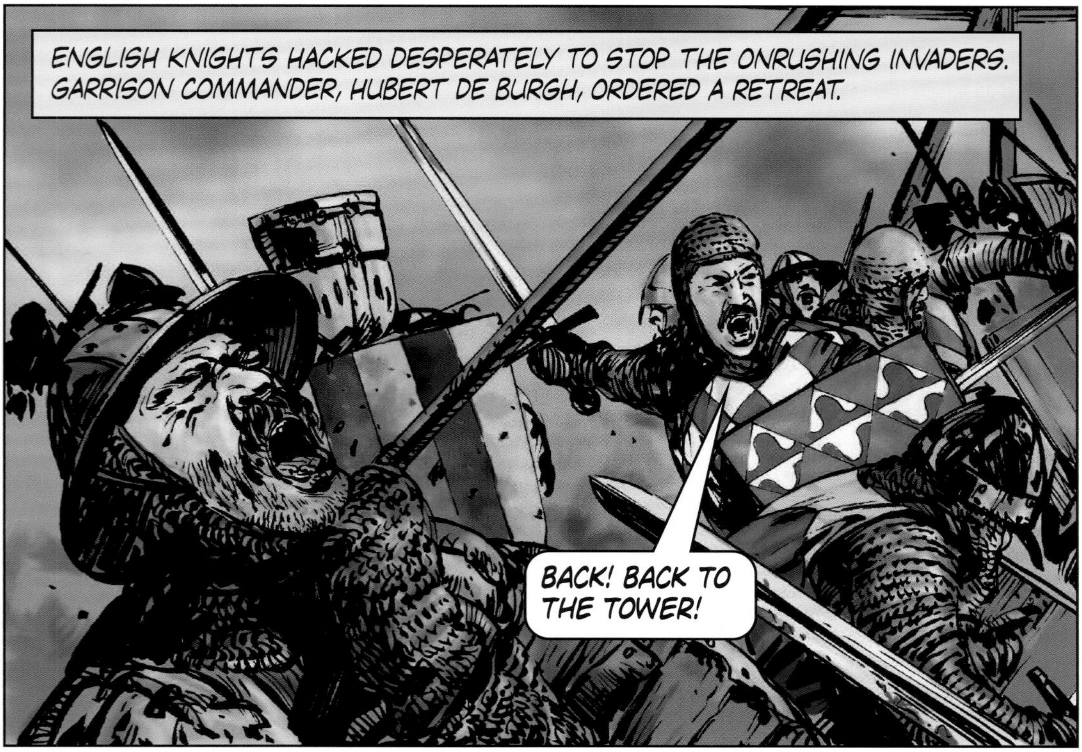
ENGLISH KNIGHTS HACKED DESPERATELY TO STOP THE ONRUSHING INVADERS. GARRISON COMMANDER, HUBERT DE BURGH, ORDERED A RETREAT.
BACK! BACK TO THE TOWER!

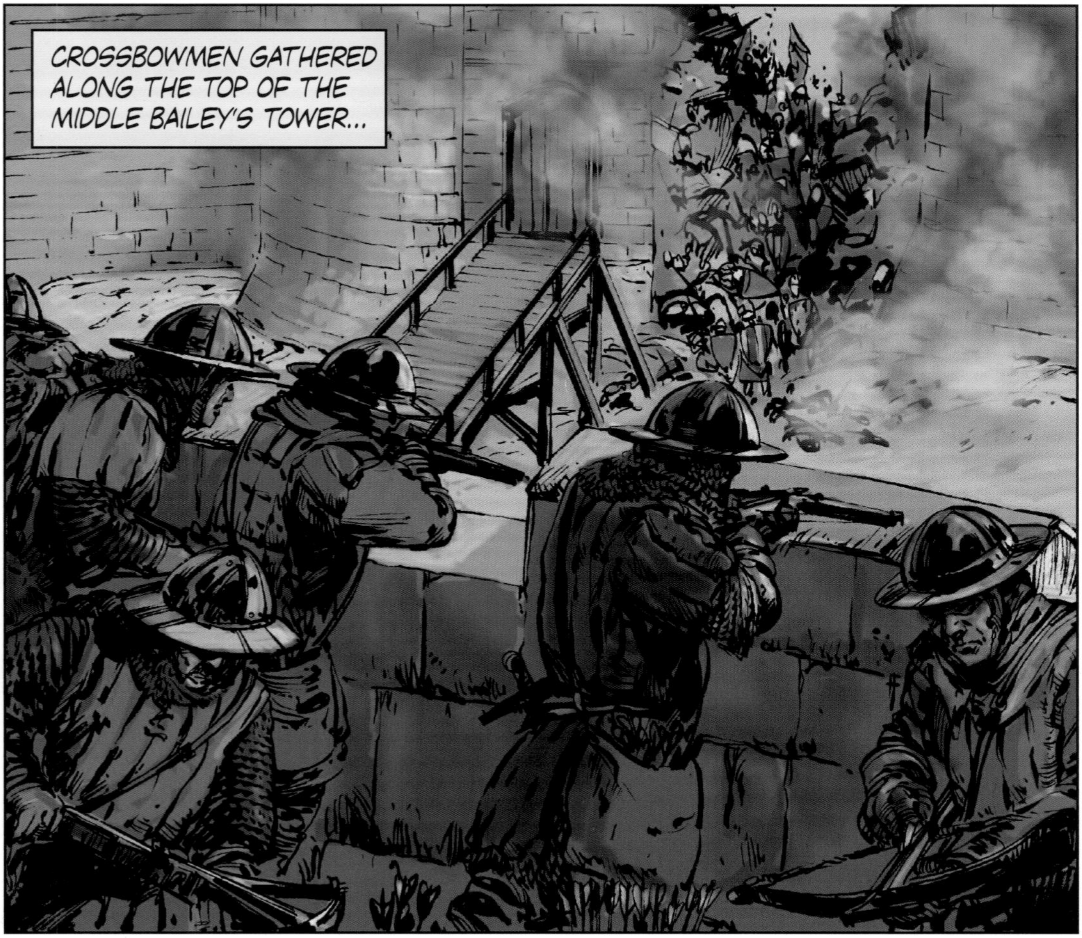
CROSSBOWMEN GATHERED ALONG THE TOP OF THE MIDDLE BAILEY'S TOWER...

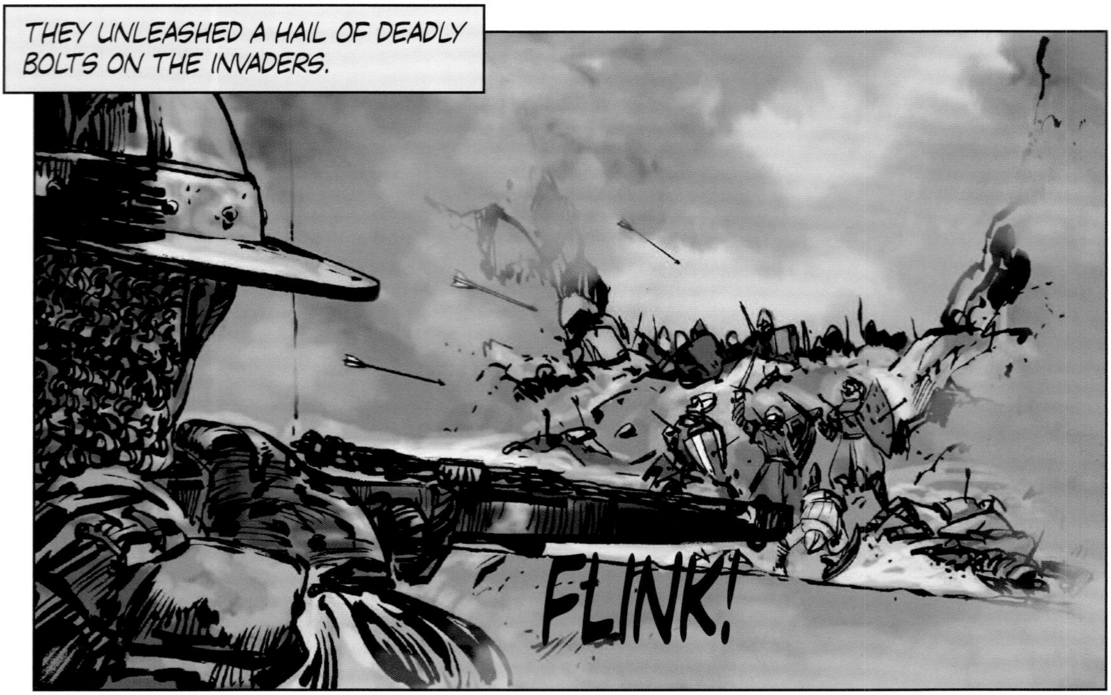
THEY UNLEASHED A HAIL OF DEADLY BOLTS ON THE INVADERS.
FLINK!

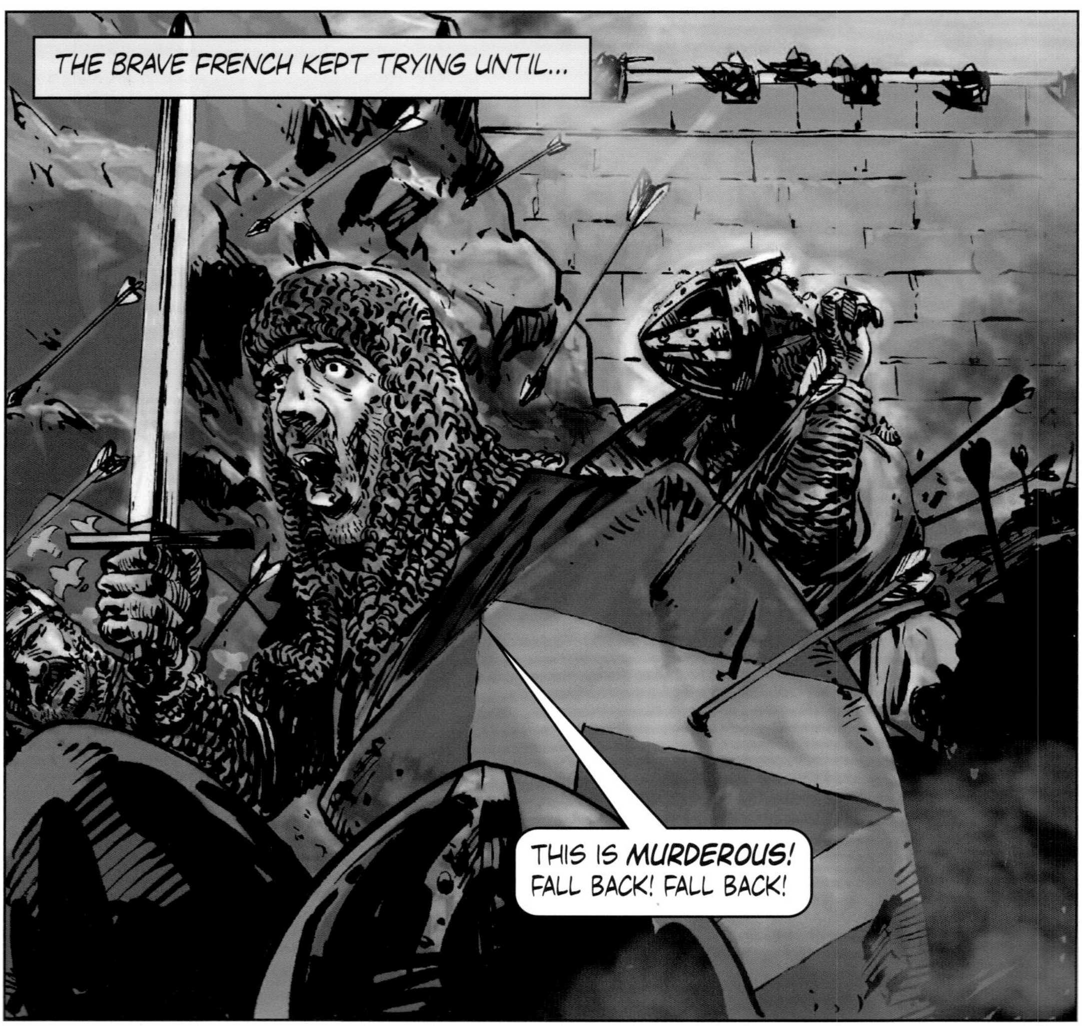
THE BRAVE FRENCH KEPT TRYING UNTIL...
THIS IS MURDEROUS! FALL BACK! FALL BACK!

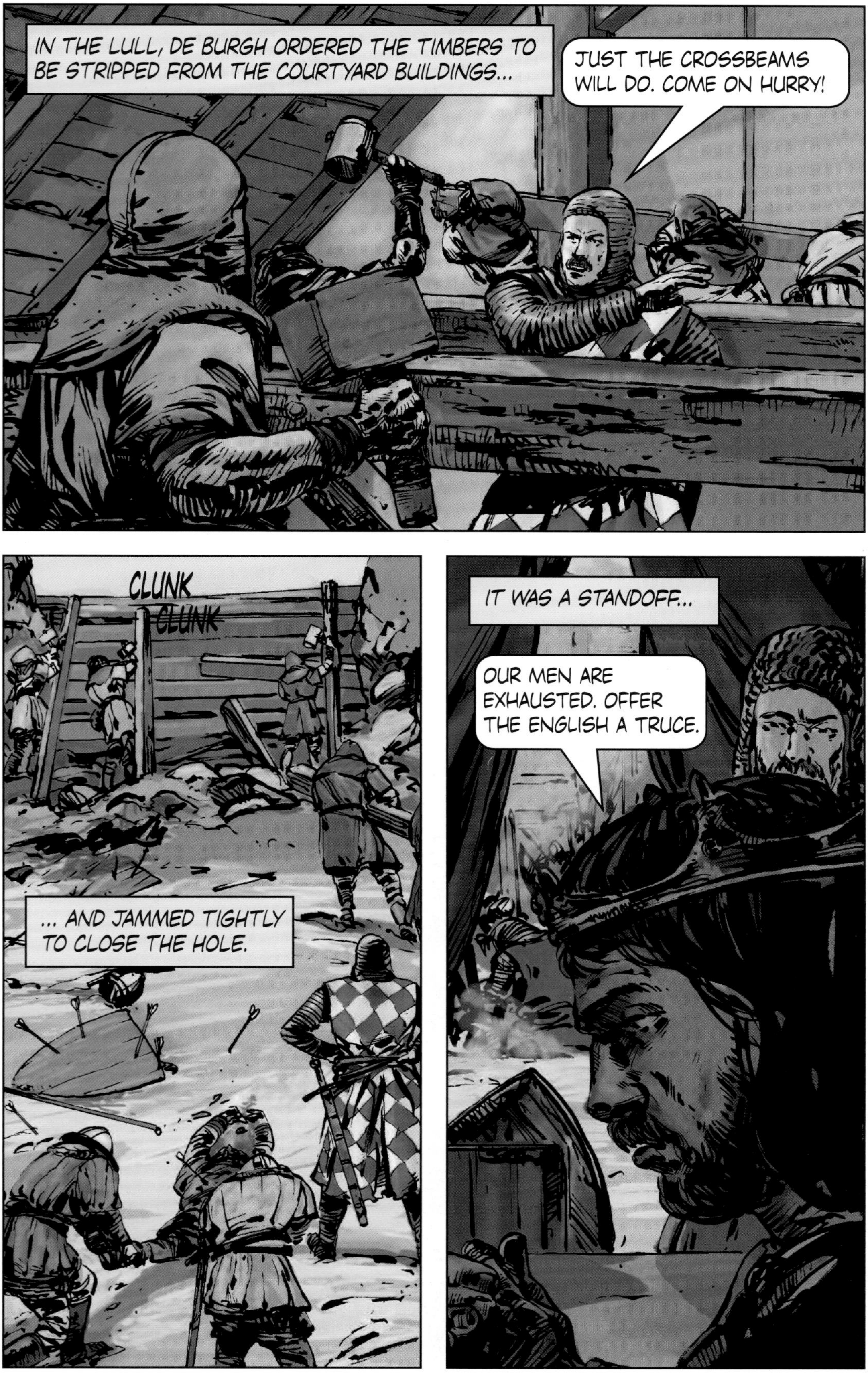
IN THE LULL, DE BURGH ORDERED THE TIMBERS TO BE STRIPPED FROM THE COURTYARD BUILDINGS...
JUST THE CROSSBEAMS WILL DO. COME ON HURRY!
CLUNK
CLUNK
... AND JAMMED TIGHTLY TO CLOSE THE HOLE.
IT WAS A STANDOFF...
OUR MEN ARE EXHAUSTED. OFFER THE ENGLISH A TRUCE.

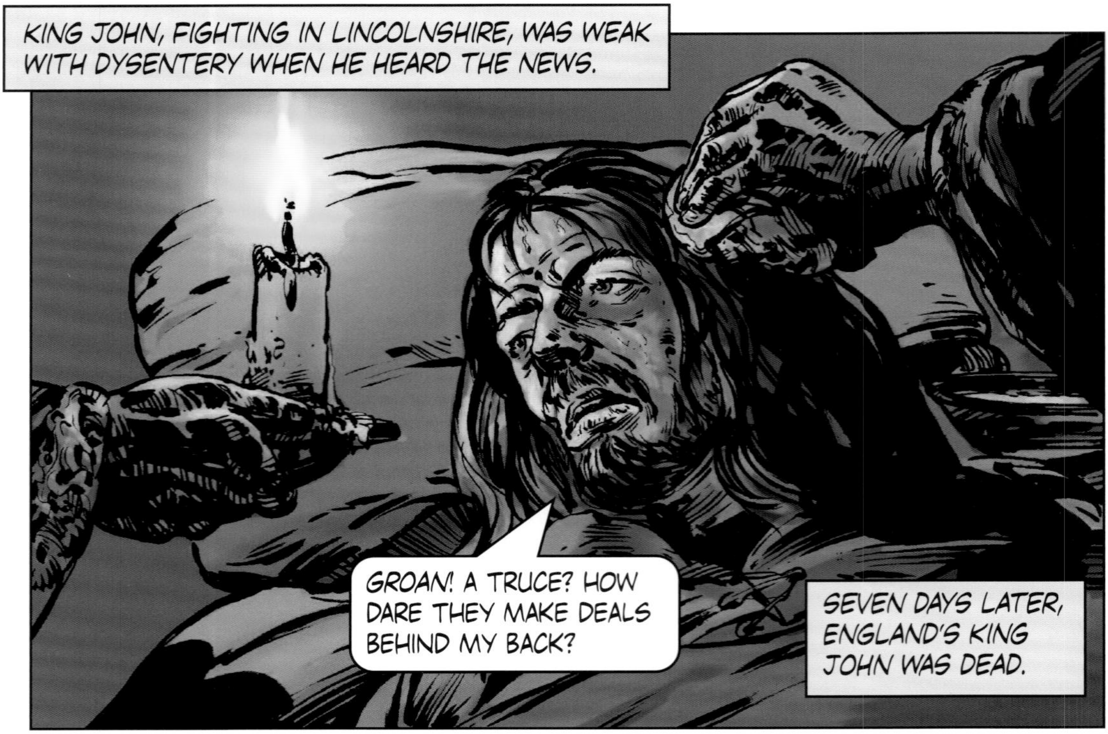
KING JOHN, FIGHTING IN LINCOLNSHIRE, WAS WEAK WITH DYSENTERY WHEN HE HEARD THE NEWS.
GROAN! A TRUCE? HOW DARE THEY MAKE DEALS BEHIND MY BACK?
SEVEN DAYS LATER, ENGLAND'S KING JOHN WAS DEAD.

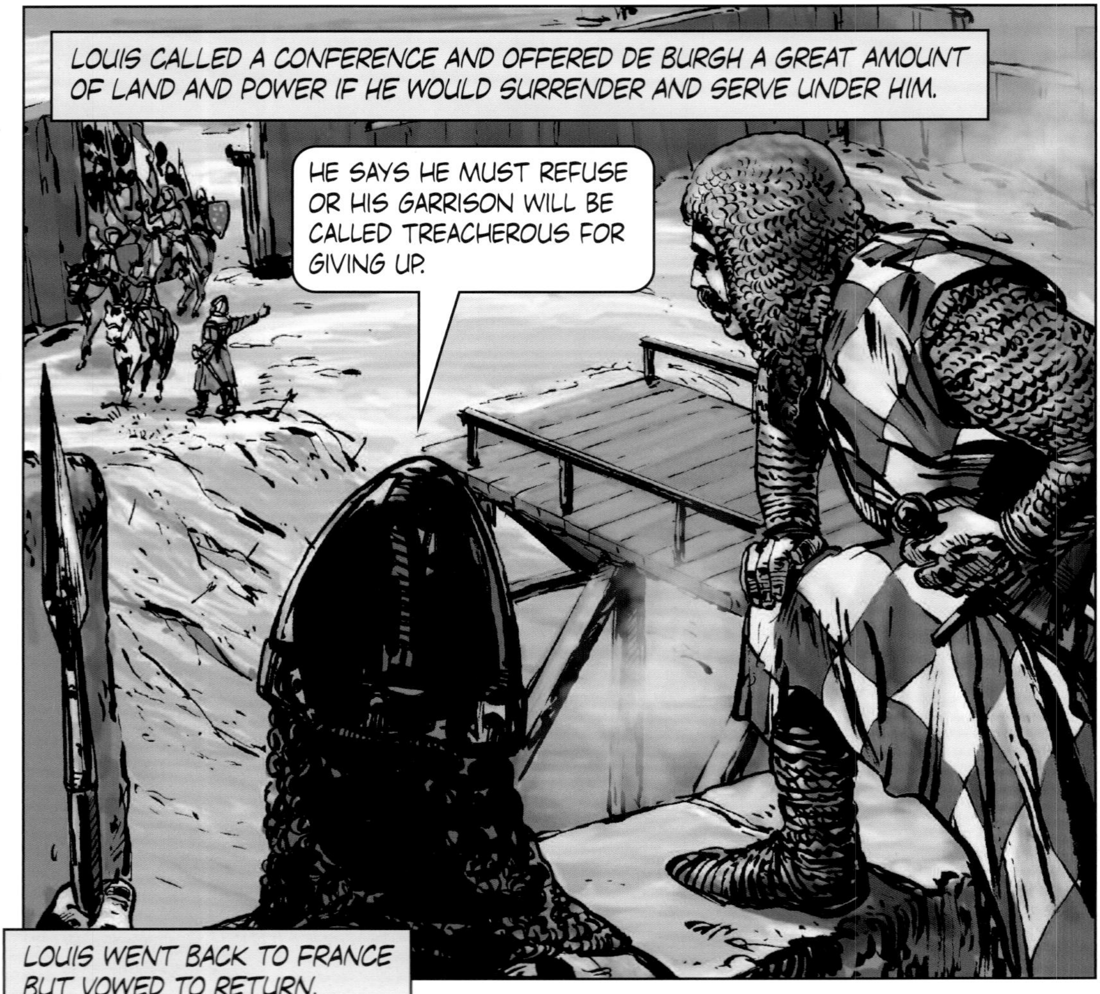
LOUIS CALLED A CONFERENCE AND OFFERED DE BURGH A GREAT AMOUNT OF LAND AND POWER IF HE WOULD SURRENDER AND SERVE UNDER HIM.
HE SAYS HE MUST REFUSE OR HIS GARRISON WILL BE CALLED TREACHEROUS FOR GIVING UP.
LOUIS WENT BACK TO FRANCE BUT VOWED TO RETURN.

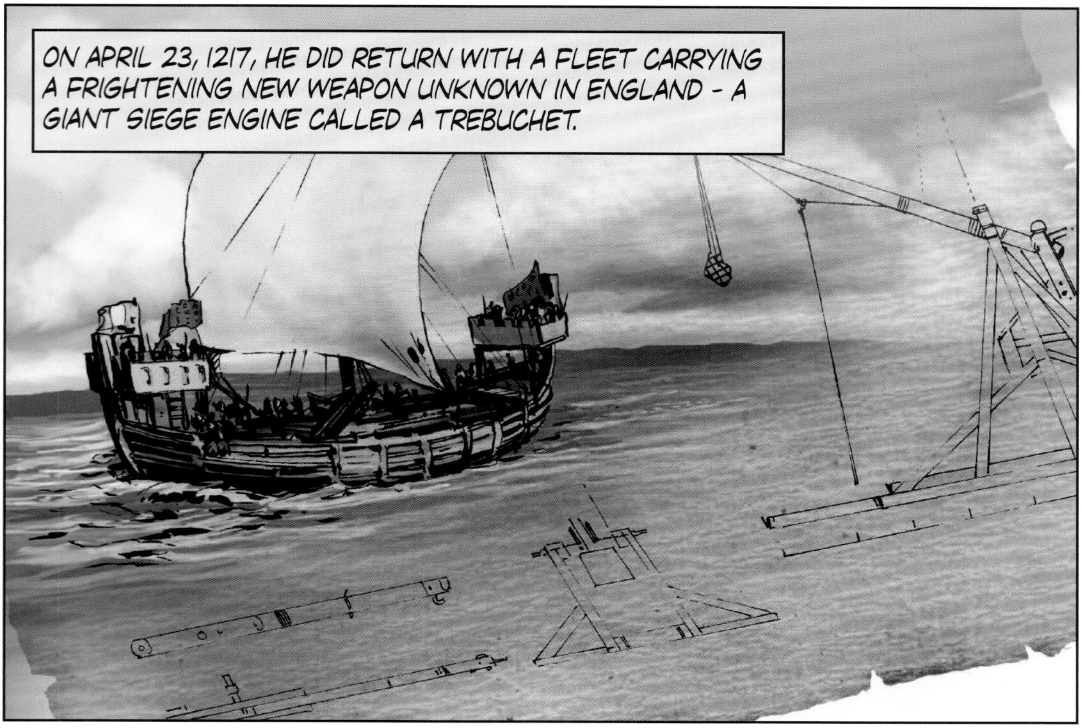
ON APRIL 23, 1217, HE DID RETURN WITH A FLEET CARRYING A FRIGHTENING NEW WEAPON UNKNOWN IN ENGLAND - A GIANT SIEGE ENGINE CALLED A TREBUCHET.

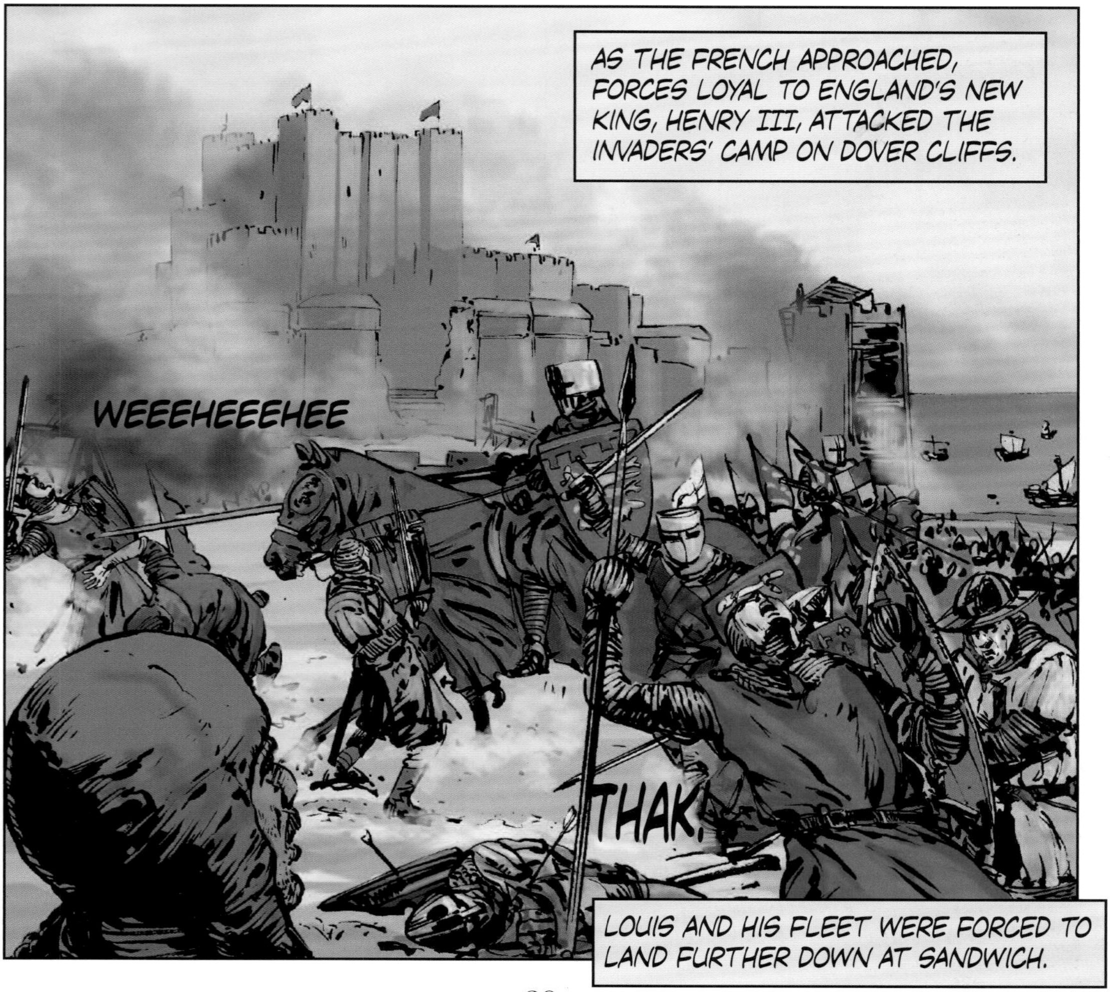
AS THE FRENCH APPROACHED, FORCES LOYAL TO ENGLAND'S NEW KING, HENRY III, ATTACKED THE INVADERS' CAMP ON DOVER CLIFFS.
WEEEHEEEEHEE
THAK!
LOUIS AND HIS FLEET WERE FORCED TO LAND FURTHER DOWN AT SANDWICH.

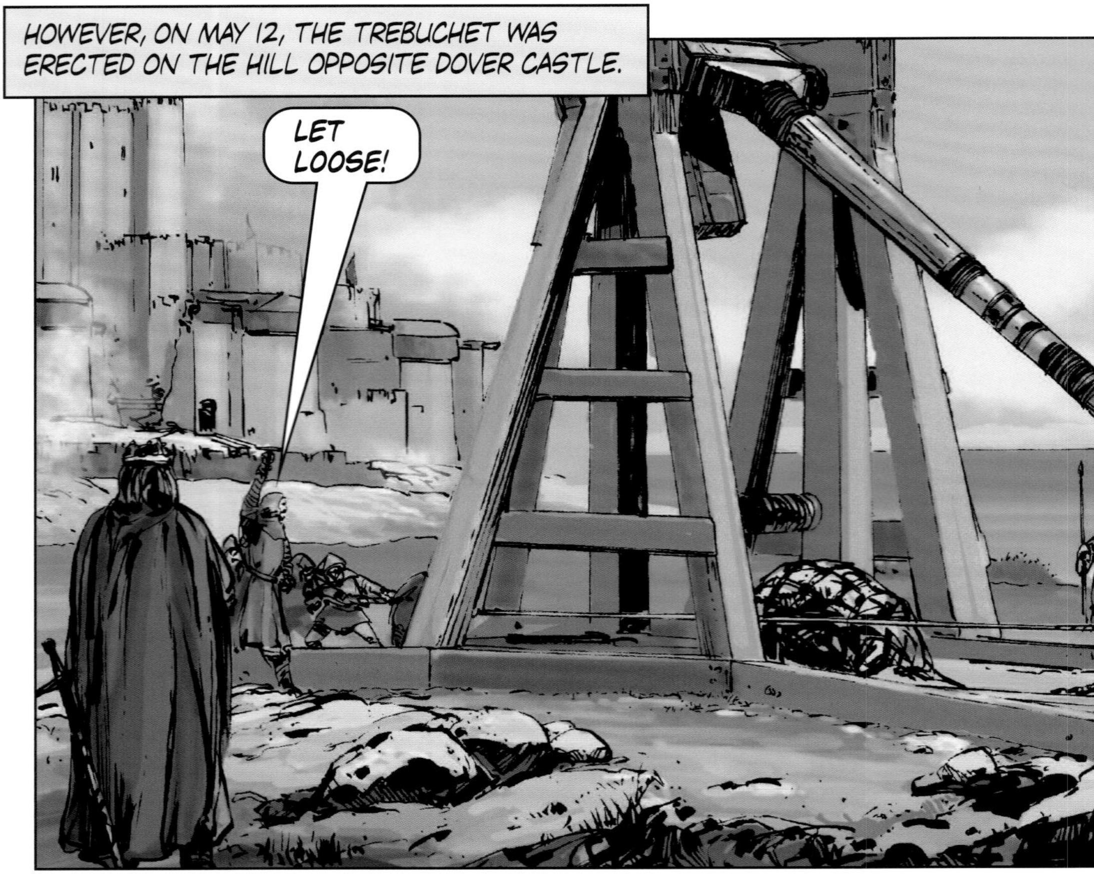
HOWEVER, ON MAY 12, THE TREBUCHET WAS ERECTED ON THE HILL OPPOSITE DOVER CASTLE.
LET LOOSE!

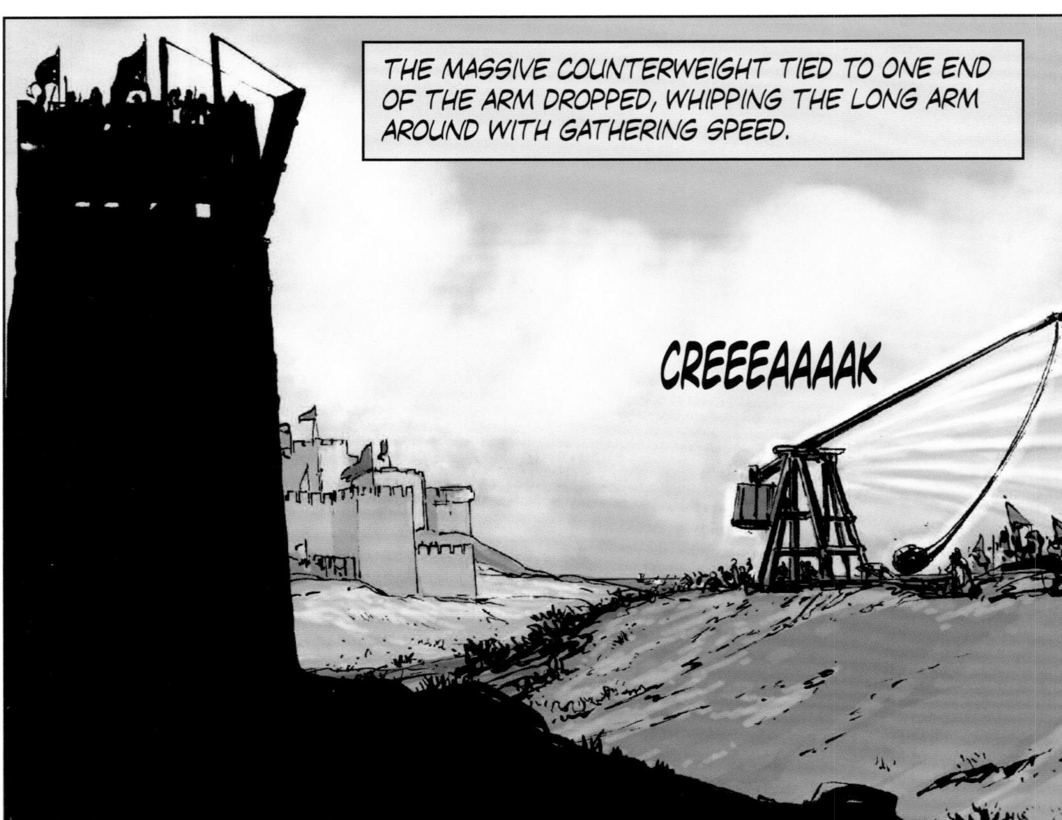
THE MASSIVE COUNTERWEIGHT TIED TO ONE END OF THE ARM DROPPED, WHIPPING THE LONG ARM AROUND WITH GATHERING SPEED.
CREEEAAAAK

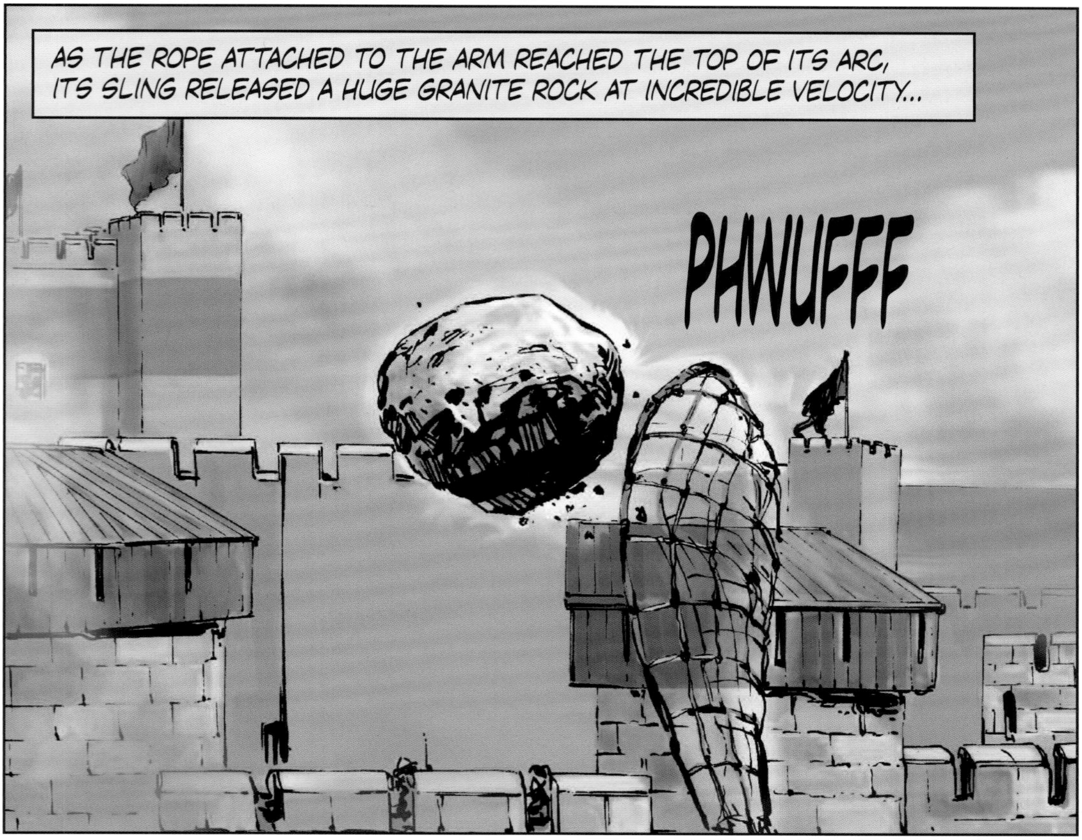
AS THE ROPE ATTACHED TO THE ARM REACHED THE TOP OF ITS ARC, ITS SLING RELEASED A HUGE GRANITE ROCK AT INCREDIBLE VELOCITY...
PHWUFFF

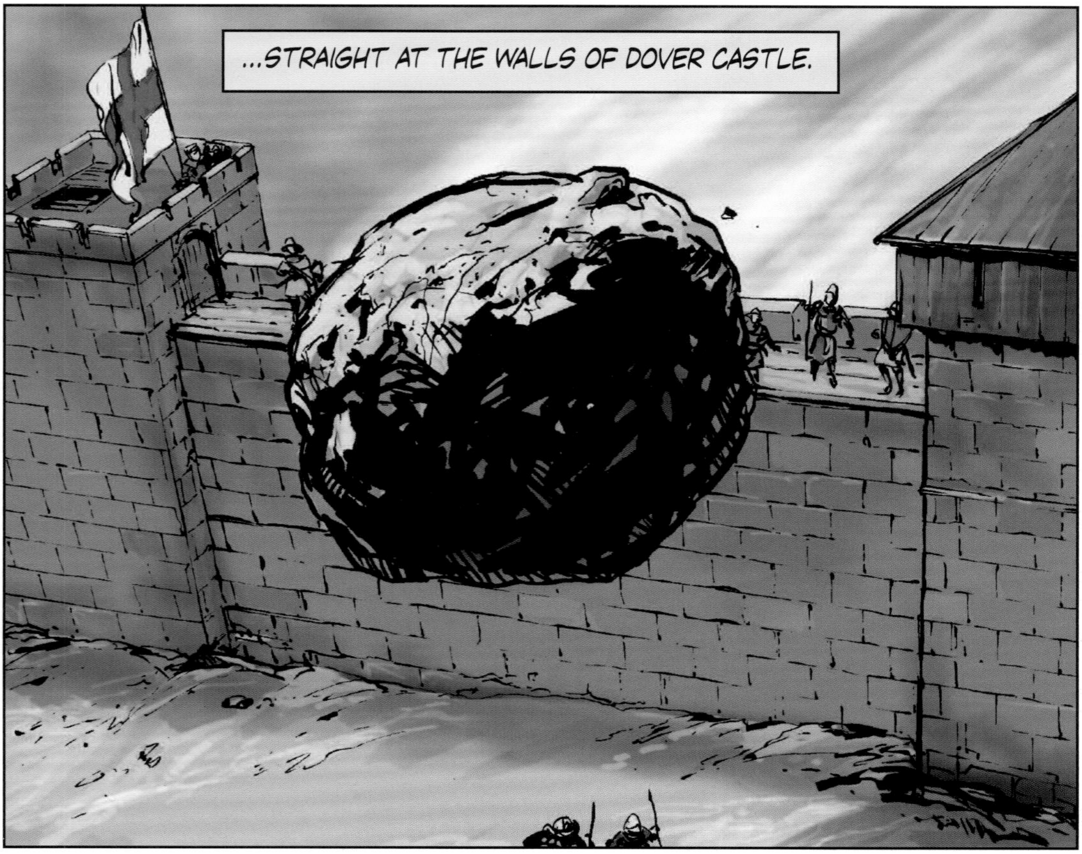
...STRAIGHT AT THE WALLS OF DOVER CASTLE.

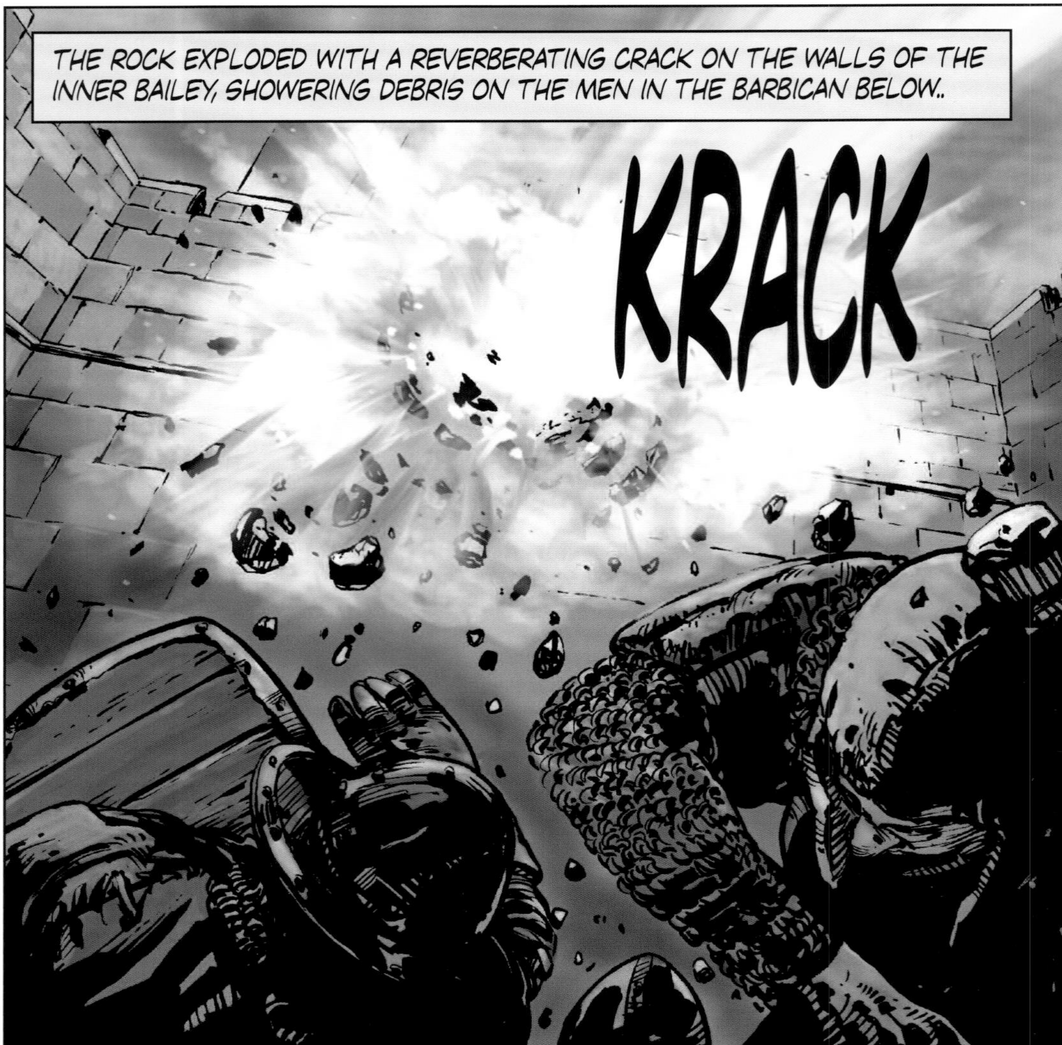
THE ROCK EXPLODED WITH A REVERBERATING CRACK ON THE WALLS OF THE INNER BAILEY, SHOWERING DEBRIS ON THE MEN IN THE BARBICAN BELOW..
KRACK

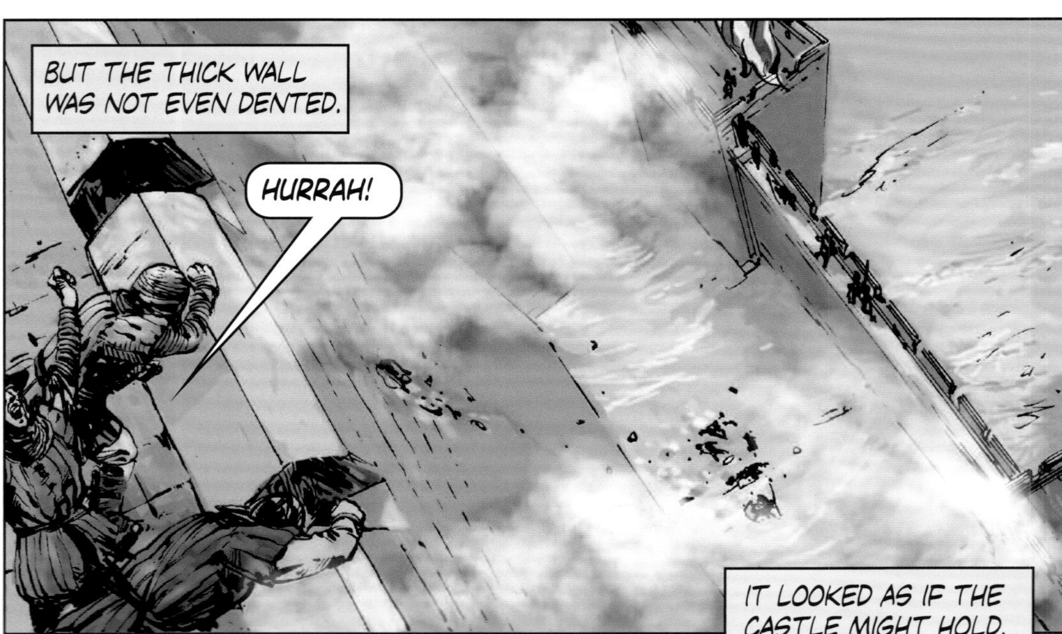
BUT THE THICK WALL WAS NOT EVEN DENTED.
HURRAH!
IT LOOKED AS IF THE CASTLE MIGHT HOLD.

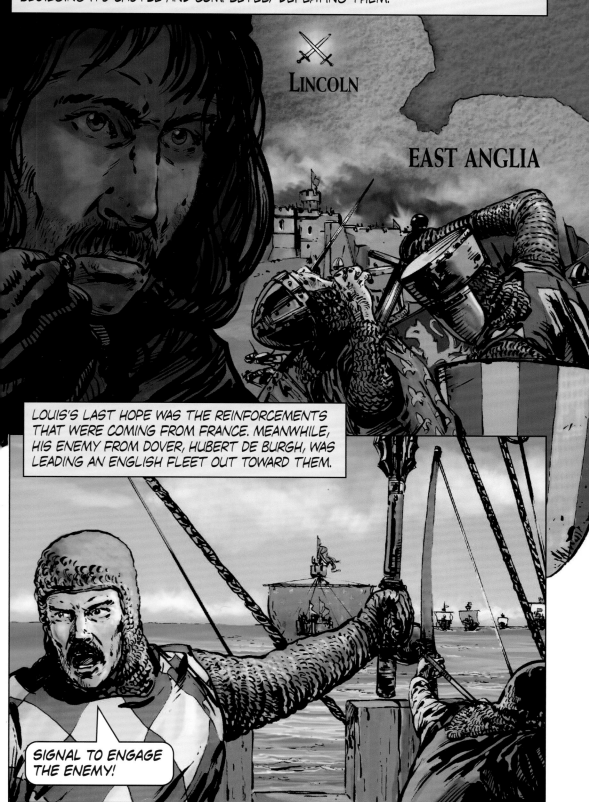

WHILE LOUIS VAINLY ATTEMPTED TO BREACH DOVER CASTLE, DISASTER STRUCK AT LINCOLN. ENGLISH SOLDIERS LAUNCHED A SURPRISE ATTACK ON THE FRENCH, BESIEGING ITS CASTLE AND COMPLETELY DEFEATING THEM.

LINCOLN

EAST ANGLIA

LOUIS'S LAST HOPE WAS THE REINFORCEMENTS THAT WERE COMING FROM FRANCE. MEANWHILE, HIS ENEMY FROM DOVER, HUBERT DE BURGH, WAS LEADING AN ENGLISH FLEET OUT TOWARD THEM.

SIGNAL TO ENGAGE THE ENEMY!

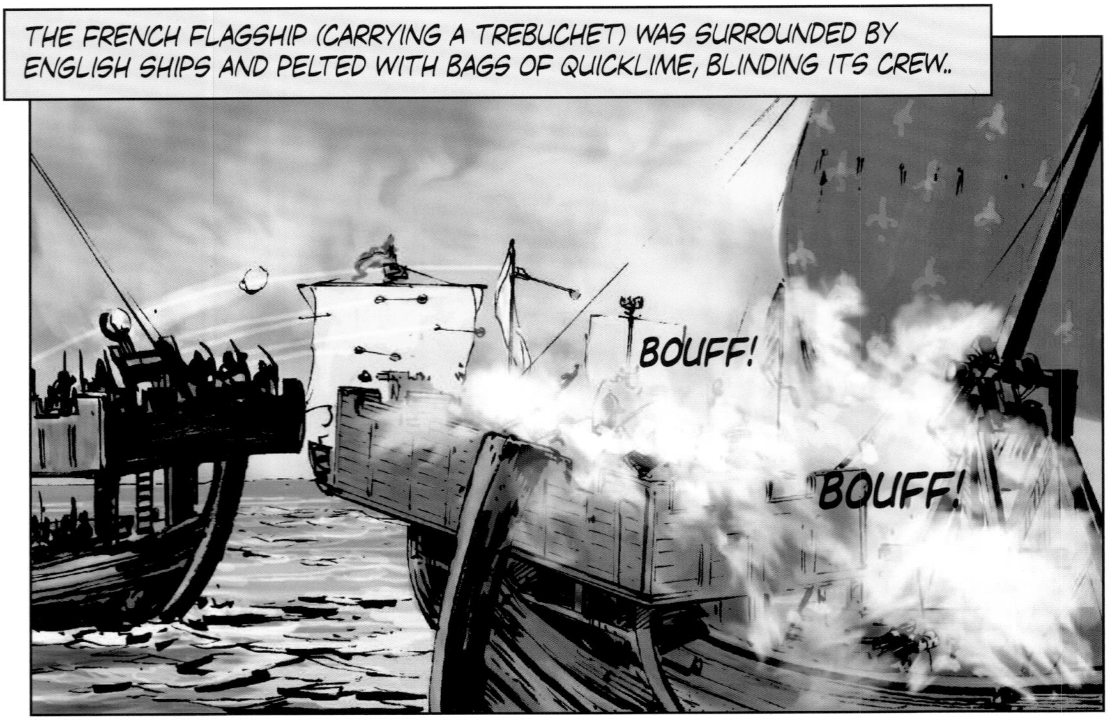
THE FRENCH FLAGSHIP (CARRYING A TREBUCHET) WAS SURROUNDED BY ENGLISH SHIPS AND PELTED WITH BAGS OF QUICKLIME, BLINDING ITS CREW..
BOUFF!
BOUFF!

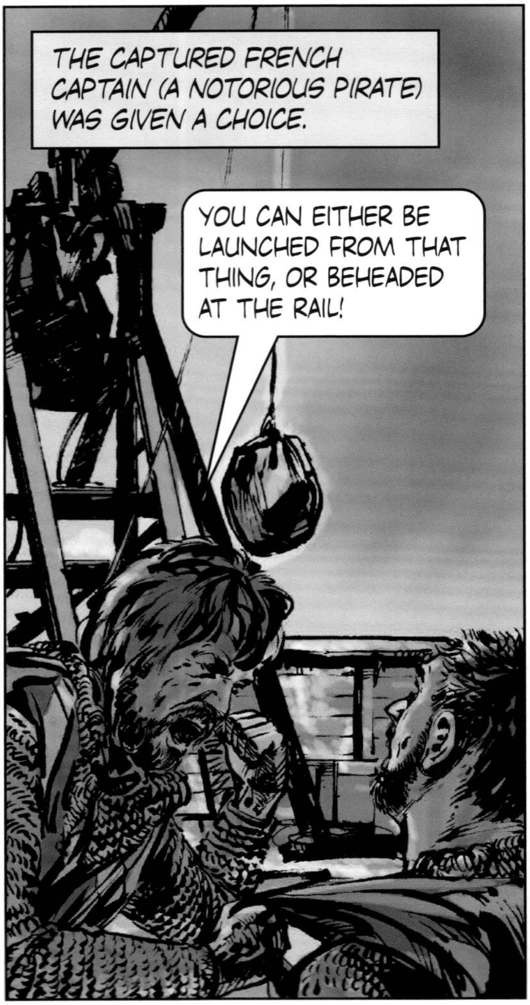
THE CAPTURED FRENCH CAPTAIN (A NOTORIOUS PIRATE) WAS GIVEN A CHOICE.
YOU CAN EITHER BE LAUNCHED FROM THAT THING, OR BEHEADED AT THE RAIL!

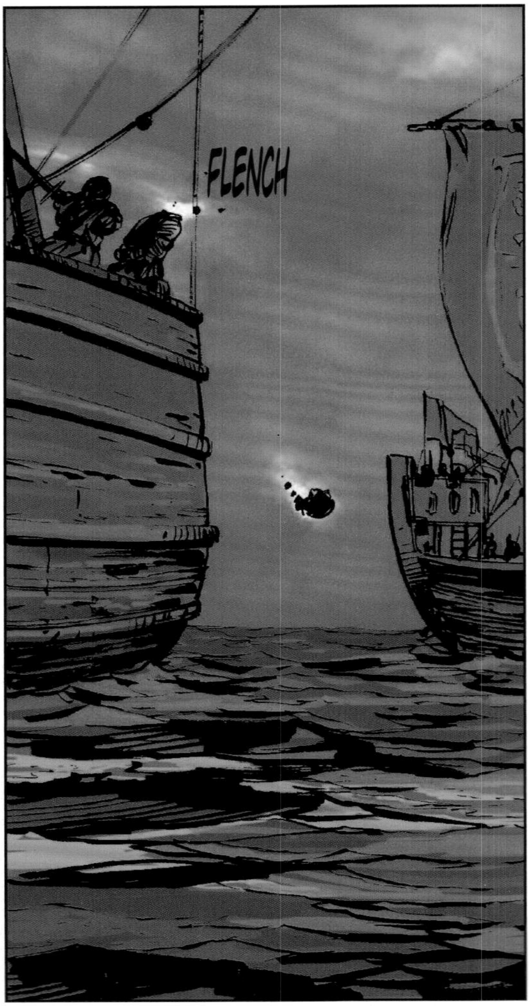
FLENCH

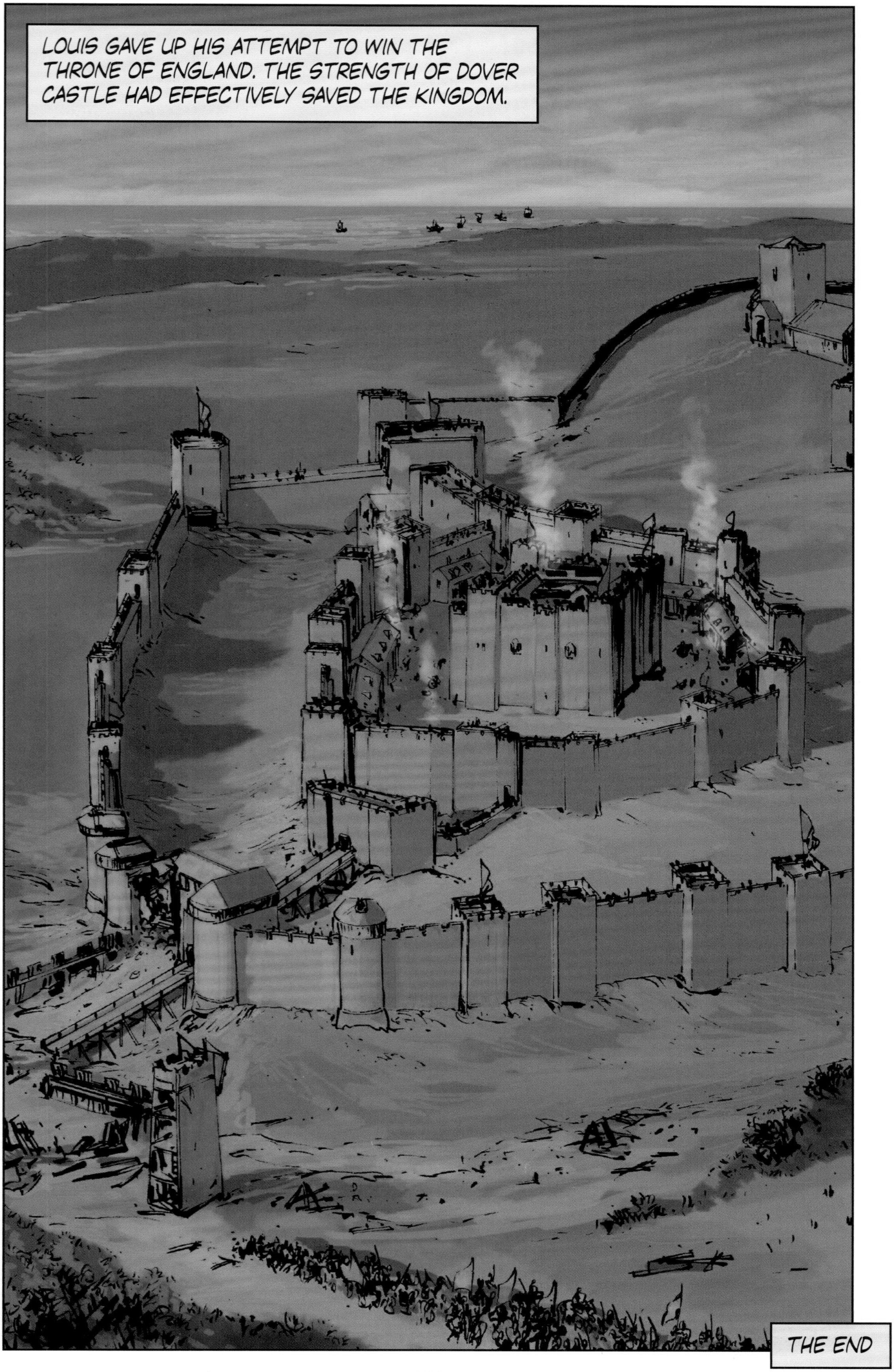
LOUIS GAVE UP HIS ATTEMPT TO WIN THE THRONE OF ENGLAND. THE STRENGTH OF DOVER CASTLE HAD EFFECTIVELY SAVED THE KINGDOM.
THE END

Edward I Conquers Wales

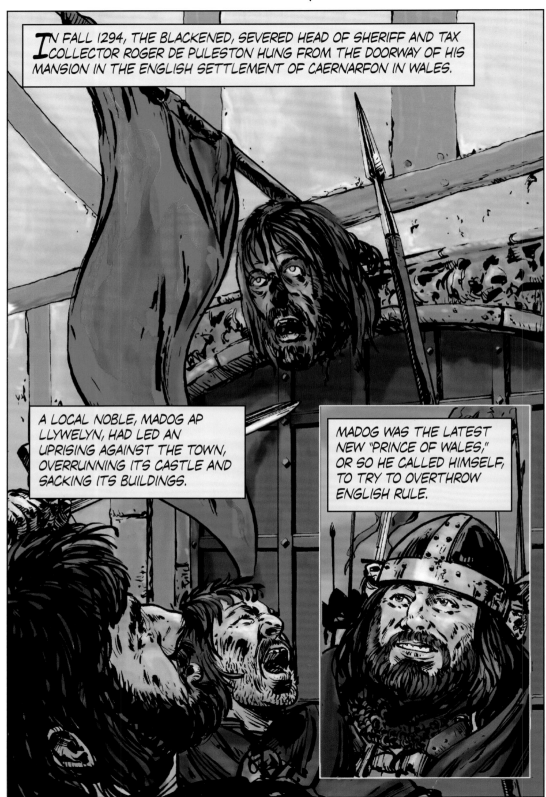

IN FALL 1294, THE BLACKENED, SEVERED HEAD OF SHERIFF AND TAX COLLECTOR ROGER DE PULESTON HUNG FROM THE DOORWAY OF HIS MANSION IN THE ENGLISH SETTLEMENT OF CAERNARFON IN WALES.

A LOCAL NOBLE, MADOG AP LLYWELYN, HAD LED AN UPRISING AGAINST THE TOWN, OVERRUNNING ITS CASTLE AND SACKING ITS BUILDINGS.

MADOG WAS THE LATEST NEW "PRINCE OF WALES," OR SO HE CALLED HIMSELF, TO TRY TO OVERTHROW ENGLISH RULE.

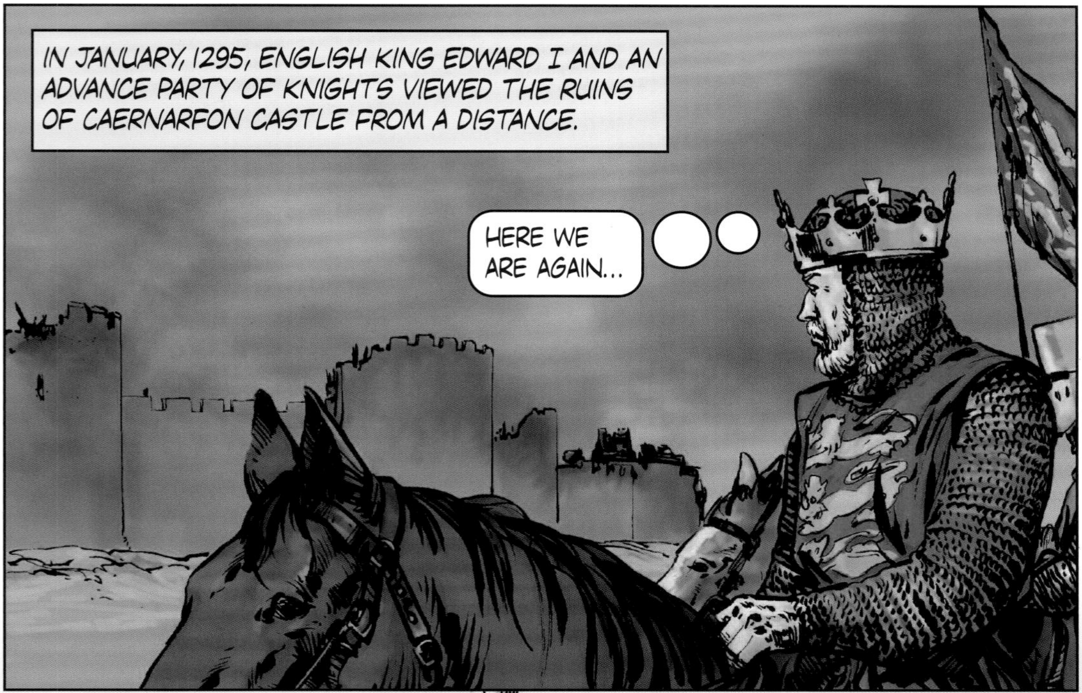
IN JANUARY, 1295, ENGLISH KING EDWARD I AND AN ADVANCE PARTY OF KNIGHTS VIEWED THE RUINS OF CAERNARFON CASTLE FROM A DISTANCE.
HERE WE ARE AGAIN...

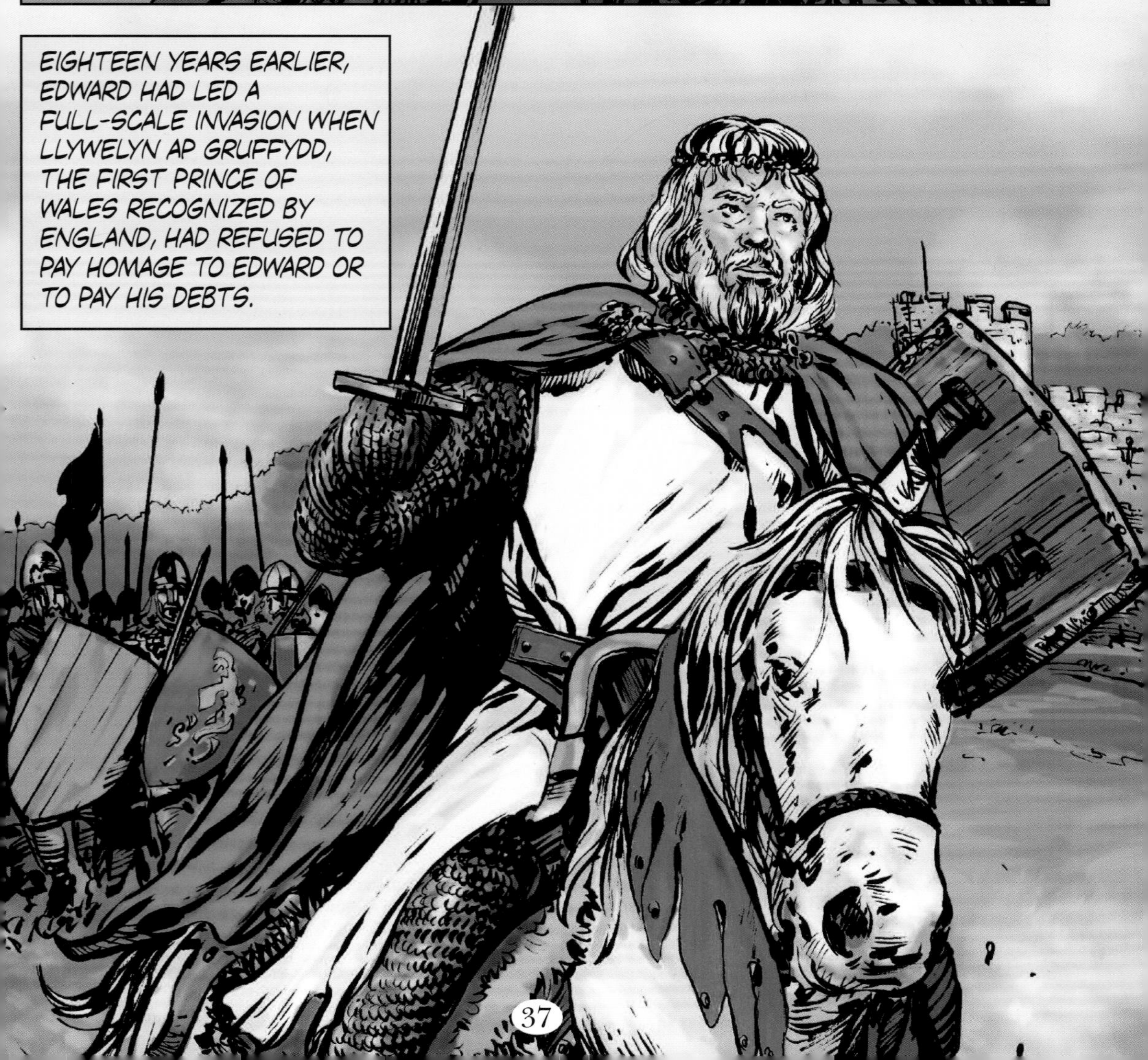
EIGHTEEN YEARS EARLIER, EDWARD HAD LED A FULL-SCALE INVASION WHEN LLYWELYN AP GRUFFYDD, THE FIRST PRINCE OF WALES RECOGNIZED BY ENGLAND, HAD REFUSED TO PAY HOMAGE TO EDWARD OR TO PAY HIS DEBTS.

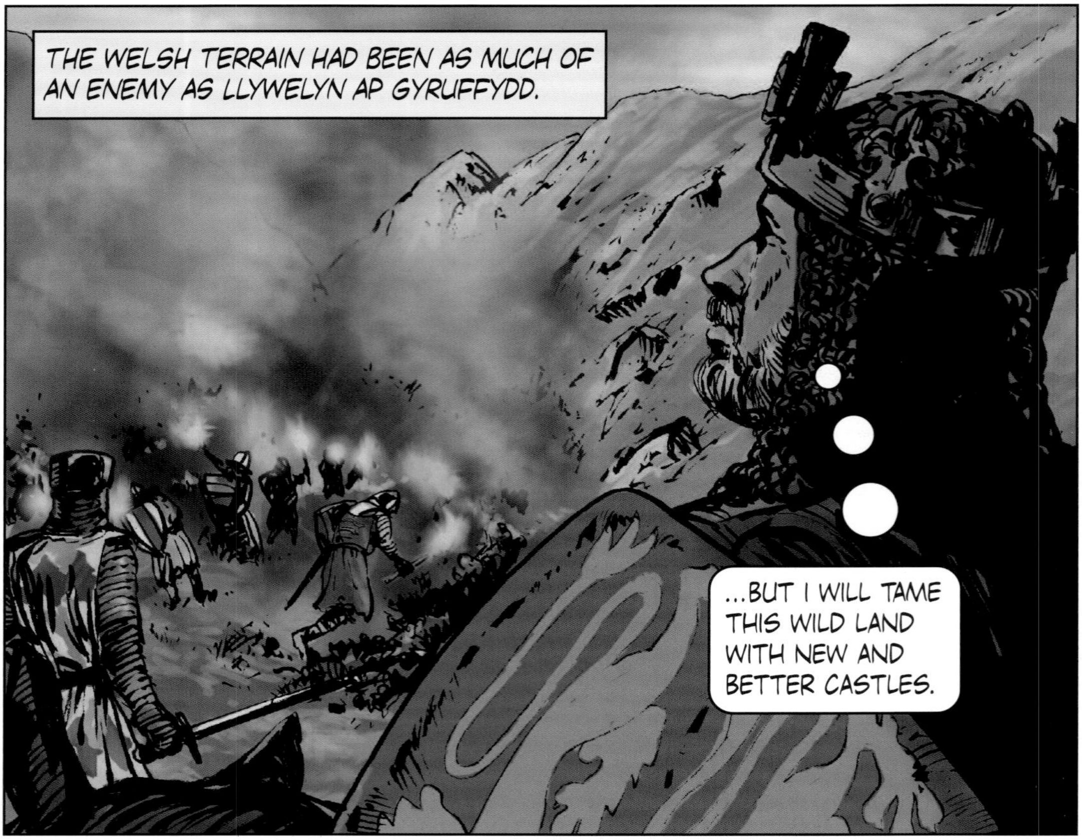
THE WELSH TERRAIN HAD BEEN AS MUCH OF AN ENEMY AS LLYWELYN AP GYRUFFYDD.
...BUT I WILL TAME THIS WILD LAND WITH NEW AND BETTER CASTLES.

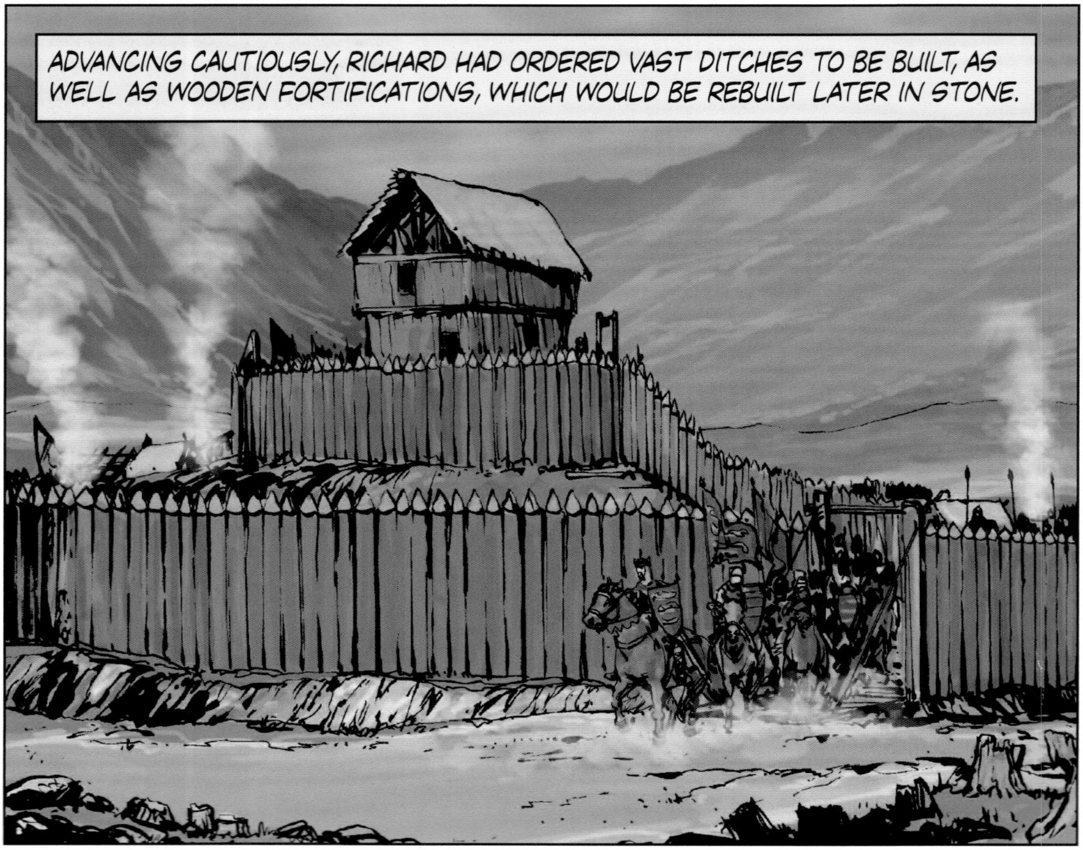
ADVANCING CAUTIOUSLY, RICHARD HAD ORDERED VAST DITCHES TO BE BUILT, AS WELL AS WOODEN FORTIFICATIONS, WHICH WOULD BE REBUILT LATER IN STONE.

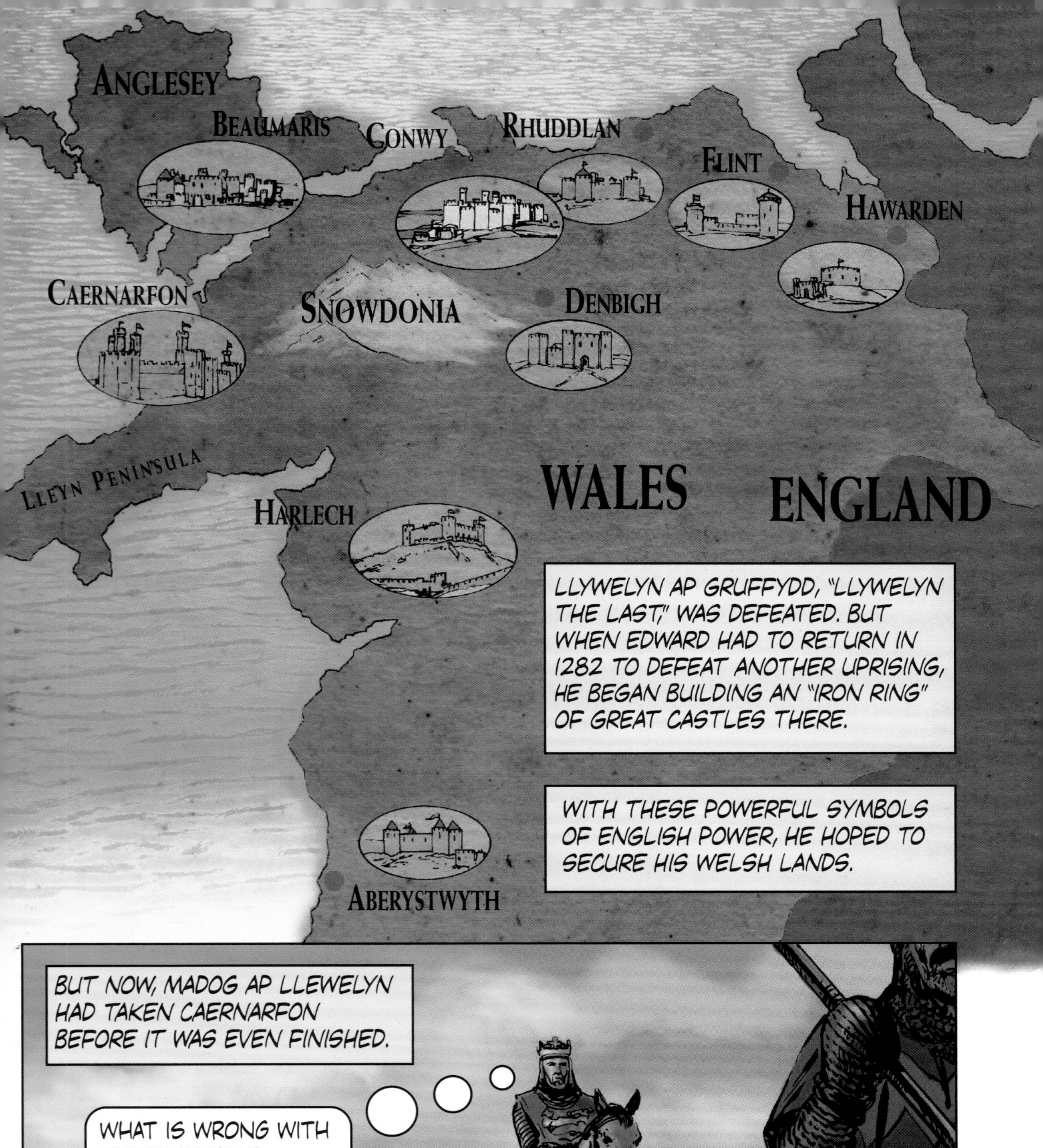
ANGLESEY
BEAUMARIS
CONWY
RHUDDLAN
FLINT
HAWARDEN
CAERNARFON
SNOWDONIA
DENBIGH
LLEYN PENINSULA
WALES
ENGLAND
HARLECH
LLYWELYN AP GRUFFYDD, "LLYWELYN THE LAST," WAS DEFEATED. BUT WHEN EDWARD HAD TO RETURN IN 1282 TO DEFEAT ANOTHER UPRISING, HE BEGAN BUILDING AN "IRON RING" OF GREAT CASTLES THERE.
WITH THESE POWERFUL SYMBOLS OF ENGLISH POWER, HE HOPED TO SECURE HIS WELSH LANDS.
ABERYSTWYTH

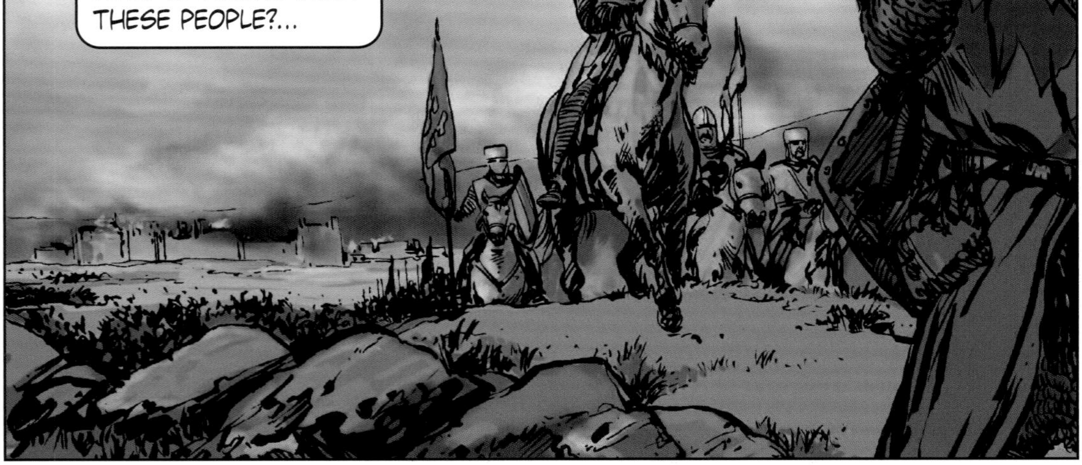
BUT NOW, MADOG AP LLEWELYN HAD TAKEN CAERNARFON BEFORE IT WAS EVEN FINISHED.
WHAT IS WRONG WITH THESE PEOPLE?...

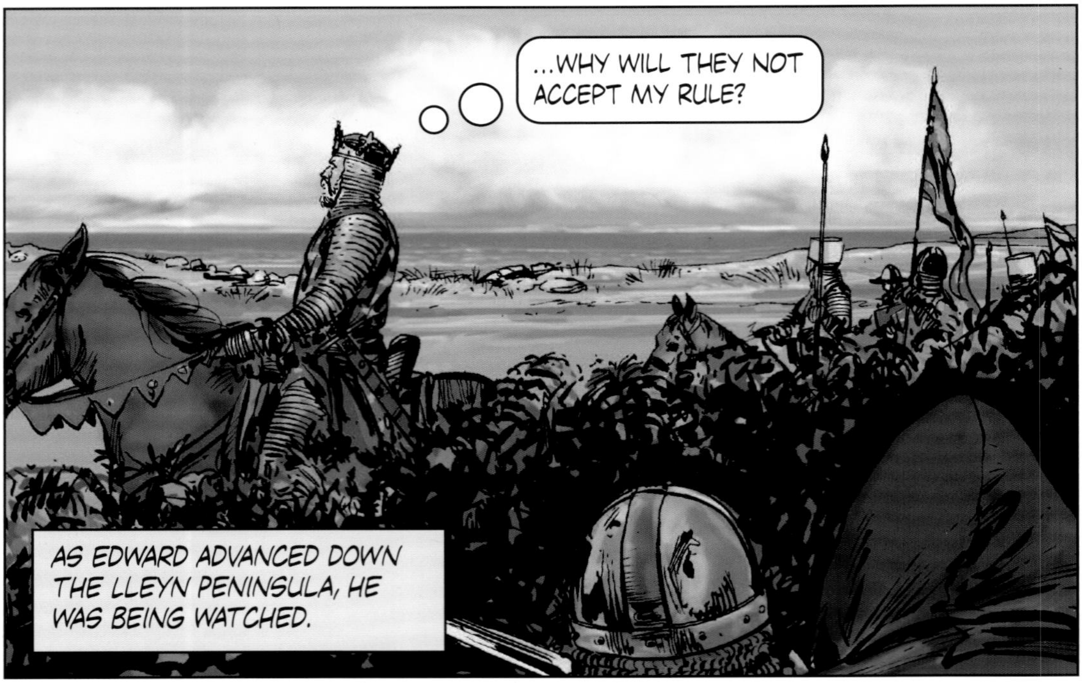
...WHY WILL THEY NOT ACCEPT MY RULE?
AS EDWARD ADVANCED DOWN THE LLEYN PENINSULA, HE WAS BEING WATCHED.

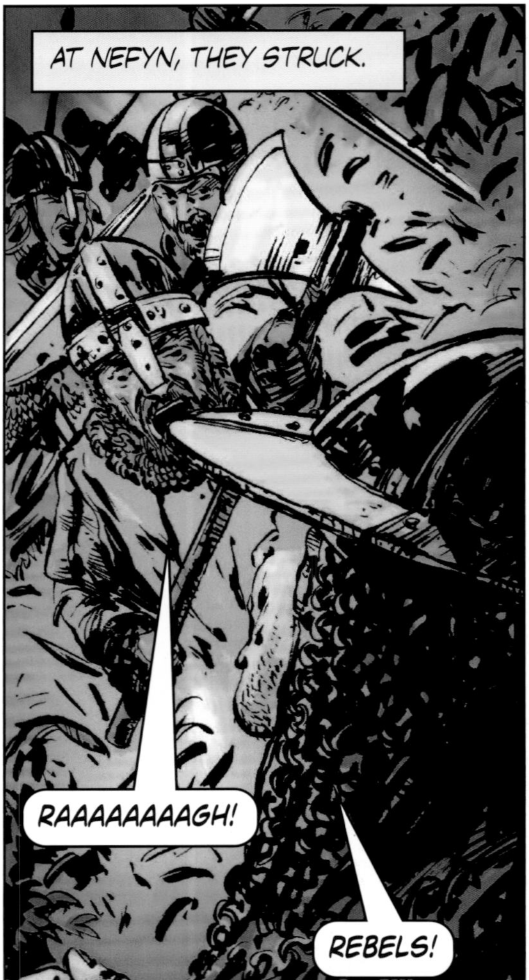
AT NEFYN, THEY STRUCK.
RAAAAAAAAGH!
REBELS!

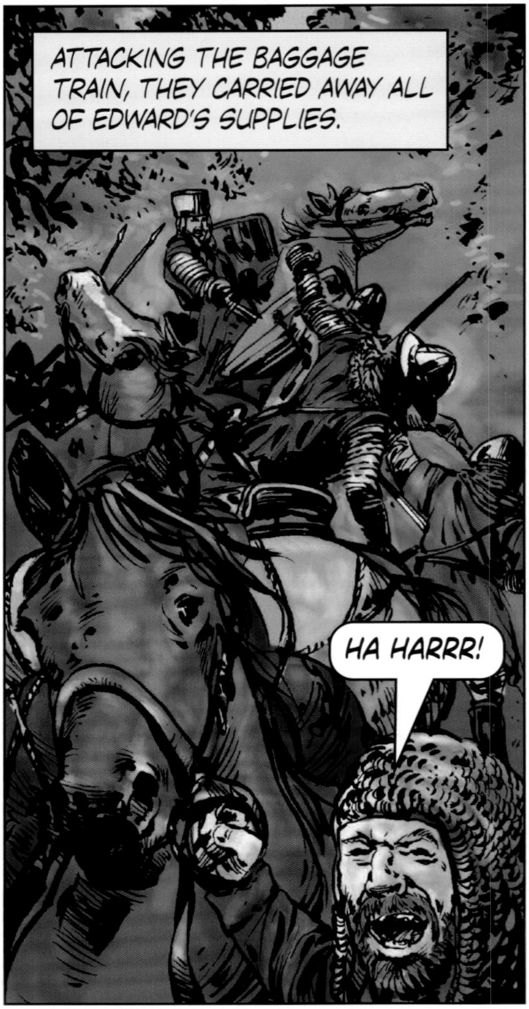
ATTACKING THE BAGGAGE TRAIN, THEY CARRIED AWAY ALL OF EDWARD'S SUPPLIES.
HA HARRR!

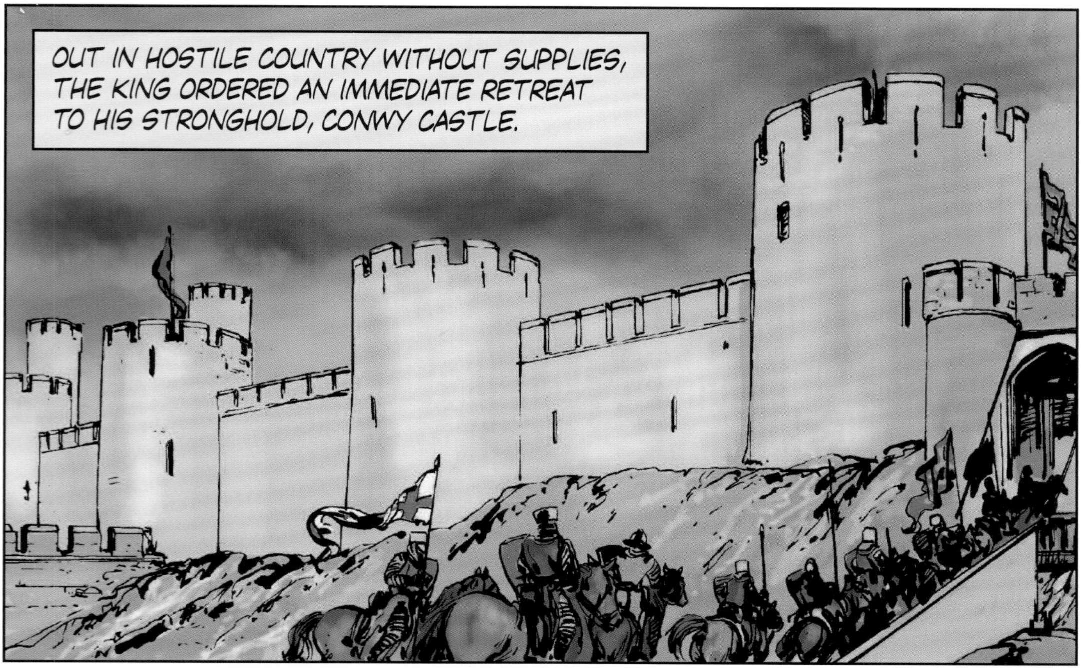
OUT IN HOSTILE COUNTRY WITHOUT SUPPLIES, THE KING ORDERED AN IMMEDIATE RETREAT TO HIS STRONGHOLD, CONWY CASTLE.

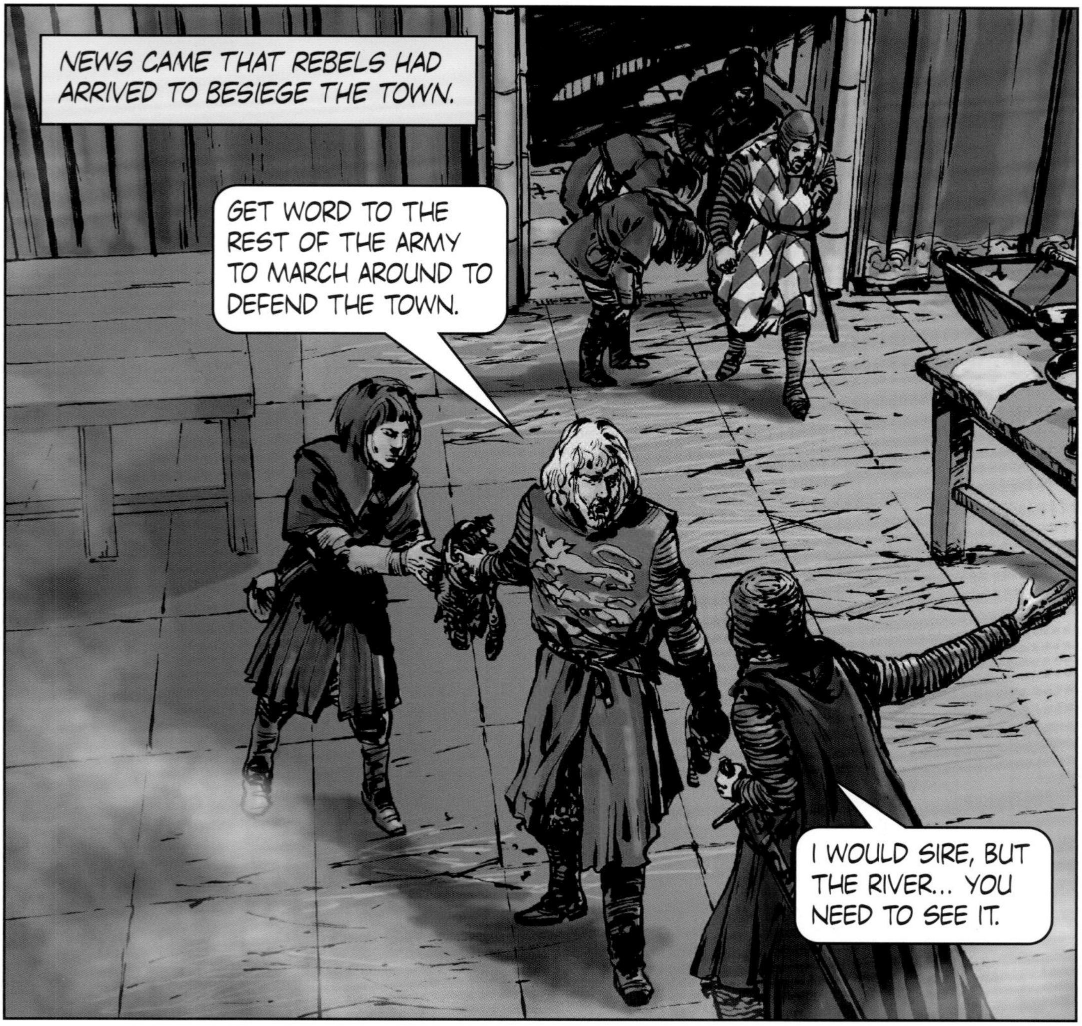
NEWS CAME THAT REBELS HAD ARRIVED TO BESIEGE THE TOWN.
GET WORD TO THE REST OF THE ARMY TO MARCH AROUND TO DEFEND THE TOWN.
I WOULD SIRE, BUT THE RIVER... YOU NEED TO SEE IT.

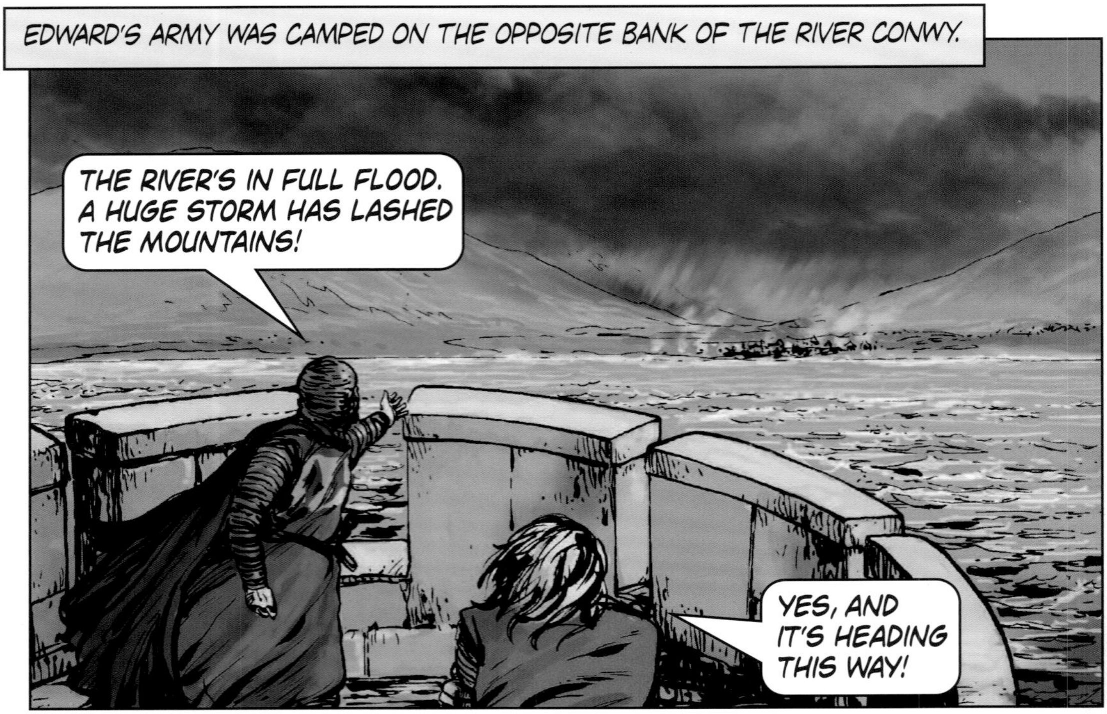
EDWARD'S ARMY WAS CAMPED ON THE OPPOSITE BANK OF THE RIVER CONWY.
THE RIVER'S IN FULL FLOOD. A HUGE STORM HAS LASHED THE MOUNTAINS!
YES, AND IT'S HEADING THIS WAY!

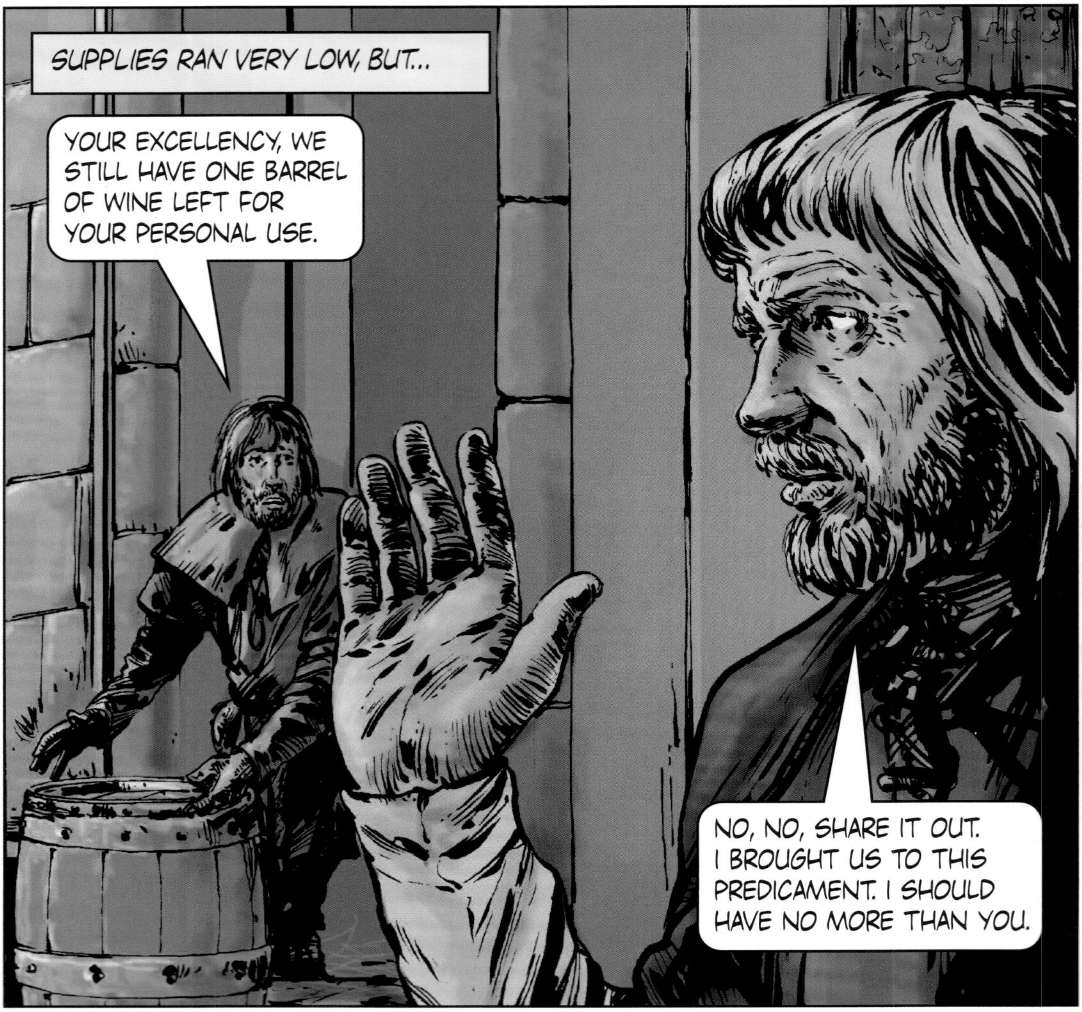
SUPPLIES RAN VERY LOW, BUT...
YOUR EXCELLENCY, WE STILL HAVE ONE BARREL OF WINE LEFT FOR YOUR PERSONAL USE.
NO, NO, SHARE IT OUT. I BROUGHT US TO THIS PREDICAMENT. I SHOULD HAVE NO MORE THAN YOU.